THE
PERFECT
HERETICS

by
JEFF MERRIFIELD

The Perfect Heretics by Jeff Merrifield
with contributions from Anne Brenon, Michel Roquebert, Yves Rouquette, Nicolas Gouzy
Translations by Marie-Ange Chevrier, Audrey Wagner, RogerDepledge
used with permission and with acknowledgement to Editions Loubatières, Privat & Perrin
Designed and typeset by John Maynard
Photographs by Alan Dearling (black & white printing by Ian Leonard)
Illustrations by Simonne Dearing
Published by Enabler Prublications, 3 Russell House, Lym Close, Lyme Regis, Dorsett DT7 3DE, UK
ISBN 0 9523316 2 4
June 1995

THE PERFECT HERETICS

by
JEFF MERRIFIELD

with illustrations
by
Simonne Dearing

photographs
by
Alan Dearling

contributions
from
Anne Brenon
Michel Roquebert
Yves Rouquette
Nicolas Gouzy
translations by Marie-Ange Chevrier

An Enabler Publication

Contents

PREFACE

I first encountered the Cathars when a friend lent me a book.

The friend: Ken Campbell, esteemed theatrical guru, founder of the Science Fiction Theatre of Liverpool and legendary Fortean seeker. The book: 'Flicker' by Theodore Roszak.

There are some books you flip through, some you read in fits and starts and some that are hard to put down. This book changed my life.

'Flicker' is ostensibly about films, particularly the romance of discovering old films, black and white classics, deep films with subtitles, rare, mysterious, magical movies. I was immediately hooked by Roszak's clever use of linking the romantic notion of film to the actual romances of his main character. I could identify with that. At college, I used to run the Film Society and I knew only too well the thrill of the discovery of all those great filmic masterpieces. Truffaut, Pasolini, Bunuel, John Ford, Howard Hawks. Discovering such stuff seemed much more likely to improve the chances of real life romance. I mean, girls who liked New Wave films, weren't half attractive.

I was locked into the story before me, whisked on a roller coaster journey, joining Roszak's protagonist on a mission to find out an obscure and mysterious film-maker, whose films appeared to have a strange effect on people, causing them to feel sexual urges, but putting them off sex. I was drawn ever deeper into a world of intrigue, of 'light and dark', Maltese-crosses, 'sallyrands', and Cathars.

The word leapt out from the page at me - Cathars. It was the first time I had consciously encountered it, but it seemed familiar, enigmatic, attractive, and sad.

I particularly felt sad when I got to the end of the book, even feeling just a bit cheated. For the book had not ended as I might have wanted it to - it more fizzles out than thrusts to an exciting climax. But that was not the end of the matter. I now had a thirst, a desire to know more about these Cathars, a burning desire, you might say. I needed to find out who they were, what they did, why they seemed so familiar to me. I was on a mission.

Over the next two years, or so, I made frequent visits to the Pyrénées region, in the southern part of France. I saw the 'Cathar' castles. I trod the paths they trod. I devoured what few books

I could find on the subject: the intriguing Medieval thriller, 'The Holy Blood and the Holy Grail', Arthur Guirdham's stories of reincarnation, Lambert's densely academic 'Medieval Heretics'. I got into Medieval French music, started avidly reading huge swathes of French history, examining hefty books on theology and religious doctrine.

It seemed that my life had been preparing me for this. All I had done, seen, heard and read was leading me up to that moment, the moment when the word 'Cathars' would release me on an unstoppable quest.

This book is the first progress report back from the mission, a mission that is proving engrossing, fascinating, revealing, energising and enlightening. I hope you enjoy this brief report, I look forward to sending you more at some later time.

Jeff Merrifield
Great Totham
1995

INTRODUCTION

Chapter 1
WHO ARE THE CATHARS?

The word 'Cathar' brings a spark of somewhat mystified recognition to many people in the British Isles. It sort of rings a bell. But we are not too sure just what the word refers to. Is it treasure? The bloodline of Christ? Weren't they burned? 'Holy Blood, Holy Grail' has a lot to answer for.*

But just who were these Cathars? This book attempts to explore the popular concept of the Medieval 'Good People' most commonly associated with the name, to put these Cathars into an historical context, and to examine some of the associated myths and legends.

On the face of it, the Cathars were indeed Good People, actually preferring the appellations, 'Bons-Hommes' and 'Bonnes-Dames'. They were extremely devout. They abhorred the eating the meat of warm-blooded animals. They gave up their worldly possessions and became poor preachers. They were celibate and chaste. They were non-violent and peace-loving. They took the 'Lord's Prayer' as the basis of their adoration, the 'Gospel of St John' and the 'Book of Revelation' as their guiding principles. And they were burned. Not at the stake in ones or twos, but en masse in atrocious conflagrations. Whole towns and cities were subjected to rape, pillage, massacre and destruction, for simply supporting them. And all of this in the name of the Holy Catholic Church.

The most popular concept of the Cathars, tends to be the particular grouping of religious people, who lived in the Languedoc region of France, who predominantly practised their religion in the twelfth and thirteenth centuries. There is every reason to believe that Catharism was probably more widely spread geographically and over a greater period of time. However, the Cathars of the Languedoc were branded 'heretics' and were consequently subjected to gross persecution, culminating in the only crusade ever mounted against European Christians.

It was largely because of the Cathars that the infamous Inquisition came into being. Almost all the Cathar religious leaders, those easily identifiable, were executed, usually at mass burnings. Their noble supporters were either subjugated and killed in battle, or they too were

---

* In 1983, Baigent, Leigh and Lincoln scored a popular success in this country, and further afaield, with a best-selling history book, no less. 'The Holy Blood and the Holy Grail' throwing a wide net over swathes of history, drawing Merovingians, Knights Templars, a mysterious priest with unexplained wealth, holy bloodlines and, most particularly, the Cathars, into an historical detective story. It was an attractive book, that wet the appetite, but asked more questions than it anwered.

executed. The Inquisition was a sort of sweep-up operation, to root out those who had survived the initial onslaughts and were now hiding in the numerous mountain villages of the region. Initially the Inquisition seems to have taken the form of a thorough aural investigation, of communities that were suspected of having Cathar sympathies and connections. This was something akin to, and just as insidious as, the McCarthy hearings in the United States of America: do you know, or have you ever known anyone who has known, someone who is a Cathar? However, the Inquisition later became synonymous with cruel and barbaric tortures, ruthlessly applied in order to extract information from reluctant witnesses.

One thing seems absolutely sure: if you were deemed to be 'heretic', there seems to have been no limits as to what gruesome things might be done to you.

The Church of St. Serninin Toulouse, one of the places where the plot against the 'Heretics' was hatched

Chapter 2
THE NATURE OF HERESY

We tend not to hear much about heresy in common parlance. Though, interestingly, a recent series on BBC Television, about scientists with unorthodox research methods, was called 'The Heretics' and featured flames and brandings in its title sequence. By and large, the notion of heresy seems to be the province of the academic. In the cloistered environs of academia the nature of heresy, and some of the grotesque social and political responses to it, are sanitised and, consequently, given a spurious justification.

To read some of the academic versions of history, the fact of heresy seems to be ample reason for the waging of justifiable war and tends to excuse even the most barbaric acts against those adjudged to be heretic. But what is heresy?

> "A belief or practice contrary to or at variance with the orthodox doctrine of a religious system, especially a doctrine involving dissent from Christian dogma, by a professed believer."

Thus the Oxford English Dictionary, in its concise form, defines 'heresy', adding:

> "opinion of what is normally accepted unorthodoxy; free thought and free thinking."

Similarly, 'dogma' is defined as a:

> "principle, tenet, or system of these, as laid down by the authority of a Church; or, an arrogant declaration of opinion."

Leave aside the overtly religious connotations of these words and semantic analysis becomes most interesting. To be 'dogmatic' is to be regarded as stubborn and arrogantly hard-headed. To be 'heretic' is to be regarded as a free-thinker, diverging from a fixed acceptance of such hard-headed stubbornness. Hardly a reason to be burned alive.

So why were 'heretics' tortured and burned?

In order to begin to understand that, from our viewpoint at the end of the second millennium, we have to try to put ourselves into the Medieval mind, the mind of the social being at the end of the first millennium. We have to put ourselves back to a time before the world had been adequately mapped, before mass communication and the education of the common man. It is a time of superstition, insecurity and the uncertainty of even being. Where do we come

from, why are we here, where are we going? One of the few securities to be grasped at, is
the security of order. The order most easily imposed on such a world is one that originates
in grandeur and authority. These are impressive, tangible things, that can be shown to be
beneficial, not only for those who possess riches and power, but also for society at large.
Kings, lords, the Church. These are the constants in an uncertain existence. God is
omnipotent. God has ordained his bishops and monarchs to take care of our spiritual and
temporal needs here on this Earth. After all, our religious leaders are our direct link to God
and our Earthly rulers rule by Divine mandate. We must know our place in this order of things.

Our place is most probably serfdom, unless we have been lucky enough to have been born
into some noble family. We may work the land or be engaged in some useful labour, most
probably in the service of a baronial landlord. The omnipotence of God will be regularly
brought to our attention by the priests of the church. Our interpretation of the meaning of
life, if we ever think about it at all, will be filtered through this church representative. We will
have no access to the Bible, for it is written in a language different to our own, even if we could
read, anyway. Art, politics, society, life, death, the whole world in which we live is to be seen
in specifically religious terms. For that is the order of things. Our very existence is a result
of a work of Creation. Our entire social and private life centres around the idea of Salvation.
God almighty, in his heaven, who created everything. We know that one day we will die. If we
are to retain God's grace and return to his heavenly home, then we must live a good life in
the obedience service of our lords and masters and our spiritual leaders.

There is one big problem in the midst of all this order. If God is 'Good' and God created the
world, why is there such an enormous amount of 'Evil' in it? For we see famine, pestilence,
plague and innumerable wars. How can a Good God be responsible for all this? But this is
not something we should trouble ourselves with. These mighty matters are best left to our
pontiffs and rulers to sort out.

The Medieval populace were expected to sublimely acquiesce, to stew in their own ontological
angst, without complaint, if they were to attain Salvation. In the craggy villages of the
Languedoc, straggling the French and Spanish borders, in the cities of Albi, Toulouse and
Carcassonne, such existential anxiety was beginning to have an effect. It was a new
millennium. A thousand years had past since Jesus died on the Cross. The perennial promise
was of a Second Coming. People were awaiting the return of the Messiah. But he did not come.
What did come, with alarming regularity, was famine, epidemics and abject poverty. These
were seen as Divine punishments. But for what? The priests and prelates could preach forever
about 'Original Sin' and the 'Redemption of Man'. But people were beginning to grow restless,
impatient with the Church and its inability to respond to their needs.

Dogma is the strange bedfellow of heresy. In fact, for there to be heresy, there has to be
dogma. The thing that is most likely to preserve that order, to counter such restlessness, is

an even more arrogant restatement of the dogma. Dogma becomes the order that keeps our place in the system of things. One of the most important elements in this order of things is obedience. Obedience to spiritual masters. Obedience to temporal rulers. There is no doubt that at the end of the first millennium, the Church was of great importance in the lives of ordinary people. The Church was woven into the social fabric and helped medieval people define their place in the order of things. Stasis. Anything that upset this equilibrium would be more than nuisance and irritation, to those attempting to rule and minister to these societies. Free-thinking, ideas outside of the commonly accepted orthodoxy; these were dangerous tendencies.

Preachers began to appear who pointed out that the ecclesiastical hierarchy was more concerned with its own material well-being, for which it collected taxes, than with living out the strict precepts of poverty and charity laid down in the Gospels. Surely this was a precondition of a priestly life. To live as Jesus had lived. Secular prelates did not take the vow of poverty and led lives of luxury. Many priests and abbots lived permanently 'in sin' and were more renowned for their debauchery than for their religious observance.

The people began to take notice and listened to such preachings. Whilst in Rome, the Supreme Pontiff, head of the Christian church, sensing that protestations were rumbling through Christendom, but without realising how deep seated were the resentments, tried to channel the revolt by encouraging a return to spiritual values, a sort of Papal 'back to basics'. He encouraged the growth of the monastic movement, led by clergy of deep spiritual conviction, ready to undertake an inner spiritual search. They threw off the trappings of overt wealth, and trod a humble, evangelical path. Bruno of Chartreuse, Robert d'Arbrissel, Robert of Molesmes, Bernard of Clairvaux, and later, Dominic Guzman, founder of the Dominican Order and Francis of Assisi, founder of the Franciscans.

Yet the Catholic Church of Rome, despite its best endeavours, despite the very real humility of its monks, was unable to prevent the growth of anti-clerical feeling. Priests were often attacked, churches were robbed and ransacked. It was only a short step from the rejection of the messenger to the questioning of the message. Faced with a clergy that had, in many cases, become utterly hateful, new messengers of faith began to move into the limelight, exploring and rediscovering different paths to Salvation, outside the established ways of the Roman Catholic faith and openly professing doctrines that contested the dogmas of the established Church.

This was nowhere more true than in the South of France. Henry of Lausanne travelled extensively in the region, from 1116 for over twenty years, rallying the crowds with his impassioned preaching. Bernard of Clairvaux came, on behalf of the Catholic church, to speak to the same population, and was heckled out of the land. Peter de Bruys preached forcefully against the Catholic clergy and urged his supporters to violence against them. At Toulouse, in June 1119, Pope Calixtus II held a Council to anathematise certain practices in the district, of those who denied the Sacraments of the Holy Communion, rejected baptism and marriage, and disbelieved in the Priesthood and the ecclesiastical hierarchy. Such practices could not be tolerated, for they were heretical, worse they were 'Manichæn'. This was a name that came to symbolise 'heresy' for centuries to come. In coming to an understanding of the teachings of Mani, it will be necessary to look at the beginnings of the very Christian orthodoxy that allowed heresy to be identified.

A LITTLE HERETICAL MOMENT

First a little interlude. Let me be heretical for a while.

There may be a theological argument that because the Christian Church evolved by surviving horrific, savage and brutal persecutions, and by miraculously resisting the most brutal of external pressures, that it must be regarded as the true religion and we should accept it as that. Indeed, countless thousands have. However, the way it evolved proves nothing, save that it evolved in this way. It might equally have evolved in some other way, if the winks and nudges of history, and different or greater pressures had been brought to bear, for whatever practical, political and invariably spurious spiritual reasons. Like life, in fact! Life on Earth evolved in a certain way, because of certain biological chance happenings. It might equally have evolved in another way, if some of these chance happenings had worked out differently.

The theological argument no doubt follows, that Divine intervention was involved in each of the chance happenings that brought about the evolution of the human race and the rich environments of the Earth. Equally, Divine intervention could have been responsible for all those political intrigues that wrenched the orthodox church into existence, and the equally horrendous, savage and brutal persecutions it carried out in the name of Christianity. Was God so lacking in goodness that he allowed such corrupt men to make political capital in His name, at such horrendous expense of others? Could the God of Bountiful Mercy be thought to sanction the merciless killing of men, women and children, in His name?

If it is wrong to take a life, how can it be right to execute a killer? If it is wrong to reject orthodoxy, and one of the tenets of that orthodoxy is: 'Thou shalt not kill', how can it be right to burn those deemed to have veered from the orthodoxy?

It is fanatical adherence to such fundamentalist belief that leads to pronouncements such as the Fatwa, in this case a sentence of death, decreed by Islamic religious leaders against the British author Salman Rushdie, for writing a book, which they deemed to be blasphemous.

The three most prominent religions in the world today all evolved in a geographical area less than 1% of the total size of the Earth. And they have equally had their share of persecution perpetrated against them, but also have had their equal share of persecuting others, often in no less a brutal and savage way.

There! At one time, I could easily have been burned for saying such things.

ORTHODOXY
and
HERESY

Chapter 3
ESTABLISHING CHRISTIANITY

There were accusations of heresy almost as soon as there was a Christian Church. At least, from the beginning of the orthodox Christian Church. Born into a world hostile to its own being and persecuted fearfully itself, the Christian Church soon learned to fight like with like. Whilst it was persecuted from without, it soon acquired an effective knack of purging itself of heresy from within.

In order for there to be heresy, there has to be an orthodoxy to be heretical against. Unfortunately, there seems to be an underlying assumption on the part of many scholars, especially scholars of theology, that orthodox Christianity is right and that, therefore, heresy is wrong. However it is interesting to look how the orthodox Christian Church came into being.

Christianity originated in Palestine. Not a great deal is known about its founder, Jesus of Nazareth, before he began to preach in the region, aged around thirty. Palestine was a Jewish territory, under Roman occupation, on the Eastern shores of the Mediterranean. The message that Jesus brought them was one that the Jewish people had long been waiting for: 'The Kingdom of God is at Hand'.

There were many sects amongst the Jews, some chiefly spiritual, like the Essenes, others overtly political, like the Zealots. They all hoped for a long-promised Messiah, or Saviour, to liberate them from the Roman yoke. Jesus attracted large crowds with his preaching and many followed him, seeing him as the promised Messiah. But other Jews were suspicious. He preached a message of peace: "Blessed be the peacemakers," "Turn the other cheek," "Suffer the little children to come unto me." This was not the language of a revolutionary. This was not someone who was going to save the Jewish nation from oppression. His popular following soon dwindled and, eventually, he was handed over to the Roman authorities on charges of sedition. After an aural examination, the Roman Procurator, Pontius Pilate, secured his place in history by washing his hands of the matter, leaving the decision as to whether Jesus should be crucified as a revolutionary to the crowd.

The crowd chose. Jesus was crucified. A standard punishment for proven involvement in revolutionary activity. That seemed the end of the matter. Jesus' followers dispersed. Even Simon Peter, the most fervent of the disciples, had abandoned the cause. However, the faith of the disciples was restored when, as they claimed in Gospels written soon afterwards, Jesus resurrected from the dead and charged them to proclaim the good news of the 'Kingdom of Heaven' and 'Salvation of Humankind.'

The disciples of Jesus took on this apostolic mission, aiming first at their fellow Jews, but later taking the message out to the Aegean Islands, to Asia Minor, to Greece, Italy and even as far as Spain. The most prolific of these apostles was Paul, a Jewish convert from Tarsus. In all the countries the apostles first visited there were Jewish settlements and the Christian preachers usually began with these. But the Jews in general were not won over. Back in Palestine, anti-Christian riots broke out and there was a complete break when the Christians refused to support the Jews during the uprising against the Romans in AD66. For the Jews this seemed sure proof that Jesus could not have been the promised Messiah. For the Christians, a new era had begun, when even time was started again and years were measured Anno Domini.

When Josephus writes about Jesus, he uses that name, for he knows that Christ is a translation of the Messiah, so he adds a derogatory 'so-called' when he appends the name 'Christ'. When the Jews are writing about Jesus, in the Talmud, they write about him as 'the illegitimate son of a Roman soldier called Pantha, this Yesu worked magic, ridiculed the wise, seduced and stirred up the people, gathered five disciples about him and was hanged (crucified) on the eve of the Passover'.

The Synoptic Gospels - Mark, Luke, and Matthew - had appeared by the end of the first century, giving a comprehensive and somewhat similar account of the Jesus story. John was known as the Theologian and the Gospel of St John is regarded as reaching the most advanced theological state. It is also generally considered the least historically accurate. The Synoptic Gospels were originally anonymous and it is in a questionable second century tradition that they are accorded to the closest followers of Jesus. There is little doubt that the Gospels probably grew out of an oral tradition, the various stories being collected together in the closing decades of the first century. Other stories and accounts of Jesus' life and teachings were collected and written down. These have come down to us as the New Testament Apocrypha, the collection of parchments known as the Dead Sea Scrolls and those more recently discovered at Nag Hammadi.

Early Christians based their conception of the Essence of Christianity on two basic principles. Christianity encompassed the one Eternal Truth and the one Universal Salvation. Thus, the early Christians maintained that the Unity of the Church, covering a diversity of theological, institutional and worship forms, consisted not of an external constitutional or liturgical uniformity, but of a Unity of the Spirit. This is noted in the Bible, in a letter of St Paul to the Ephesians, "...in the bond of peace, just as you were called to the one hope that belongs to your call: one Lord, one Faith, one baptism, one God, and Father of us all, Who is above all, through all and in all."

The term Christianity was probably used first by Ignatius, Bishop of Antioch, just before the end of the first century. It is not a term referred to in the New Testament. The term itself is a rather late appellation, used to contrast the beliefs and way of life of Christians from those of both the Jews and the sectarian Jewish-Christians, the Christians who wished to retain the Mosaic Law. Philo of Alexandria, in the first century, gives an interpretation of the Jewish religion as 'the true philosophy'. But Justin Martyr, a mid-second century philosopher and writer, praises Christianity as "the true philosophy." He interprets philosophy as more than the 'correct manner of knowledge'. It also includes a 'correct way of life', a morality to live by. Augustine, the renowned fourth century theologian and scholar, writes that the Christian religion is 'as old as the World'. And Eusebius of Cæsarea called Christian religion 'the first, only and true religion', meaning that Christianity was inherent in the beliefs of man since the creation of the world. His linking of this view with Logos, the Word or Divine Reason, led to an identification with Christianity as the true religion - 'And the Word was God'. Clement of Alexandria, in the second century, summed up the Unity of Christianity in the phrase: 'The River of Truth is One'.

This unity of life and teaching, espoused as the Essence of Christianity in the early church, was not maintained for long. Because of the development of doctrine along the lines of true and false religion, involving relationship with numerous theological groups, the earlier and less rigid concept of Unity was displaced by a tendency towards uniformity, in the orthodox definition of Church doctrines. Theology became increasingly detached from its original concept as the Unity of the Spirit - the Essence:

> "Go, therefore, and make disciples of all Nations, baptising them in the Name of the Father, and of the Son and of the Holy Spirit, teaching them to observe all that I have commanded you."
>
> Matthew 28 vs.19-20

A missionary commandment - or the Commission of Jesus.

Christianity is not unique in promulgating a universal salvation, with such a missionary consciousness and global commission. Siddhãrtha Gautama, the Buddha, the Enlightened One, founder of Buddhism, addressed his teachings not only to fellow Indians, but to all people, some five centuries before Christ. And five centuries after Christ, Mohammed, the Arabian prophet, founder of Islam, proclaimed his Law not only to his fellow tribesmen, but also to all mankind.

Of all the world religions, only Christianity established itself as a world religion in a total geographical sense. However, the phenomena becomes quite striking when it is recognised that this expansion all over the world, commissioned by Jesus some 2,000 years ago, took place primarily within the last three centuries. Numerous times in the first 1,500 years of its existence did Christianity come near to extinction. It now has over a billion adherents, significantly greater numbers than the Islamics or the Buddhists. In the early years of

Christianity, the Church gained a footing, as it attempted to initiate the first great wave of missions, in spite of lengthy and bloody opposition from the pagan Roman Empire. It soon became the prevailing religion, not only in the Mediterranean region, but also in Syria, Egypt, North Africa, the lands around the Black Sea, Georgia, Armenia, the Persian Empire, Arabia, Abyssinia and on the Malibar Coast of India.

The Church clamped down on early controversies over charismatic leaders, controversies over heresy, persecution, political opposition, but this moved the Church severely over to a constitutional and organisational unification, pushing the notion of the Unity of Essence out of the picture. The Apostles had appointed Bishops in each of the Churches they had established, ordained by the laying on of hands, establishing an Episcopal succession. There was a definite intention in this established system of suppressing charismatic leadership and to have a uniformity of Church organisation and Christian philosophy. There was also an effort to resist dissenting interpretations of the Christian message. This lead to a unification of teaching and liturgy. Persecutions strengthened the consciousness of unity within the Church and amongst Christian communities. They mutually assisted each other through organisations concerned with those arrested, imprisoned or condemned to the horrors of labour in the mines of distant lands.

Chapter 4
A WAVE OF PERSECUTION

The Roman Empire under Nero hit a nadir of brutality and savagery. Nero himself had murdered his stepbrother Brittanicus, his mother Aggripina, his wife Octavia and his tutor Seneca. He also executed Christians. Nero was the first to sanction institutional persecution against the Christians. In order to take attention away from some of his own incompetence and excesses, he blamed the Christians for the burning of Rome in AD64 and unleashed a great wave of persecution against them. They were arrested, imprisoned, tortured, executed and often made to join the spectacle at the Roman games, where they were put into the arena with lions and other savage wild animals, to be torn apart in front of the cheering, jeering crowds.

However, Roman brutality had been allowed to go unchecked for too long and around the world there was a seething wave of resentment about the way the Romans behaved. The vicious brutality of Roman legionnaires in Britain, brought about the furious uprising under Queen Boadicea, where thousands of Roman soldiers were slaughtered. Similar uprisings happened in the East, in Armenia, and in AD66, in Judæa. As in other places the Jewish revolt was fired by Roman cruelty and stupidity. The Romans were kicked out of Palestine and did not restore a foothold for the next five years.

Nero, himself, eventually committed suicide, as his Empire crumbled around him. In an absolute proclamation of Imperial disgrace: **Damnatio Memoriæ**. His name was stricken from the record of Roman Emperors, as if he had never existed.

Though Christianity spread widely, it did so with relative slowness. Doctrines first took root amongst the Jews of Palestine and Roman authorities had difficulty in detecting the 'Christos' believers from the Orthodox Jews. It soon dawned on them that the new Christian religion was somewhat mysterious, that its adherents belongs to the common classes and as a religion without national ties, unlike the ethnic basis of Jewish faith, Christianity posed a greater threat. Official policy was to be suspicious. Tacitus wrote, early in the first century, that there dwelt in Christians, "hatred of human kind."

The Christians did not participate in the Jewish revolt of AD66, consequently alienating themselves further from the Jews. Christianity was in the process of completely severing itself from its Jewish origins.

When the Roman army, under Titus Flavius, retook Jerusalem, in AD70, over a million Jews were reportedly killed and the rest expelled from the city, forbidden under pain of death to return. The Holy City of Judaism was destroyed. A statue of Hadrian was erected over the site

of the Temple and the city's name was changed to Aelia Capitolina. The Romans also desecrated places venerated by Christians, building a temple on the hill of the crucifixion and in Bethlehem, where the Christ child had lain. But Christians were allowed into the city.

By the end of the first century there were Christian enclaves right round the Mediterranean, including in Rome itself. It was well established and organised, with Bishops and Deacons, its own Catechism and Eucharist. Philo of Alexandria had shown that it was possible to reconcile the Christian Bible with the great Platonic ideas and there was a growing intellectual acceptance of the Christian message.

However, it was Nero who had sowed the seeds of persecution. Regardless of how discredited he was personally as Emperor, there was still an official suspicion of the spread of Christianity through the lands of the Roman Empire. Nero had blamed Christians for the fires of Rome and within fifty years the concept of Christianity as a crime was firmly established under the Flavians. Trajan ordered that Christians could be put to death, without the necessity of any other crime being levelled against them. At first, such persecutions remained local and sporadic, but under Marcus Aurelius persecution was stepped up considerably. With the Roman Empire embroiled in difficult times, Christians, who refused to make sacrifices and to participate in Imperial cults, were blamed for causing the wroth of the Gods. Under Septimius Severus the first systematic persecution was inaugurated. The arrests, tortures and executions became commonplace, as did the inclusion of Christians being savaged by wild animals at the barbaric Roman Games. These spectacles were mounted with great pomp and ceremony to prop up the Imperial position and to distract from any inadequacies of the rule. As an example of how barbaric they became, on one games day alone, 2,000 gladiators and 230 wild animals were billed to die at the 'celebration'!

Then came a more sympathetic Emperor - Diocletian. A very spiritual and superstitious man, he was at first reluctant to take action against the believers in Christ. He had thought that the Christos these people spoke of was not unlike his own Sol-God, a God of Enlightenment. He tolerated others who may worship Jupiter, or Mithras, or Seripis, why could he not tolerate those who wanted to worship Christ? It may also have been that members of Diocletian's own family had been attracted to the new religion. But pressure was placed on him from within the Imperial court. His Cæsar, or Deputy Emperor, Galerius, was the most vociferous, pointing out that many members of the Roman army were converting to the Christian faith. Eventually Diocletian put into effect the legislation that would institute what was to be the last major persecution of the Christians, issuing four specific edicts between 303 and 304. These promised that he would not spill blood, but merely arrest and imprison. When the persecution spread through the Empire, the violence was more extreme than he had ever dare anticipate. Galerius had no such scruples, decreeing that all those who would not make the pagan sacrifice and take the oath were to be burned alive. Christians were to be stripped of their possessions and put to the torture. Their Churches were to be demolished and their Sacred Books burned.

Even members of the Diocletian household were embroiled in all this mayhem. His wife and his daughter were suspected of Christian sympathies and were put to the test. They made the sacrifice and lived. However, the housemaidens were both executed, as was his trusted chamberlain, Peter. The record of his death is an example of the horrific ordeal that Christians were subjected to. He was whipped savagely, on all parts of his body, but still refusing to surrender, salt and vinegar was poured onto his torn wounds, some of which were so deep the bone was exposed. He still refused to forswear his faith, so they dragged a cooking stove under him and began to roast what was left of his body, over slow flame. They roasted just a small part at a time, ostensibly to give him every chance to submit, but more likely with the sadistic intent of prolonging his agony to the limit. Those who tortured him were under instruction to continue until he surrendered, but they continued until he died.

Prisons were filled to overflowing and new obscene implements of torture were invented daily. Those who were executed were also not forgotten by the law. In Roman law even the bodies of criminals were allowed to be buried in tombs, but there was a fear that Christian burial places might become places of veneration, so bodies were flung into the sea, weighted with stones. In the territories of Nicodemia, Syria, Phonicæa and Egypt, jails which had been built for murderers were now so full of Bishops and Priests, there was no longer room for common criminals. No one can say how many suffered martyrdom in the various provinces. Persecution was especially severe in Africa and Mauritania.

All Sacred Scriptures were garnered and burned. In a small town in the region of Phrygia, the whole population, including the curator and the municipal magistrates refused en masse to make the sacrifice. They all fled to the shelter of the Church. This made it simpler for the soldiers, who merely set fire to the Church and burned them all alive, men, women and children, and their Sacred Scriptures, all in the one fire. Such horrific methods would have been hard to excuse in time of war, but as a way of suppressing peaceful people they were inexcusable. Certainly they were alien to the ordinary administration of justice, in any state that claimed to be civilised. Even high ranking officers in the government could not escape, if they were found to have Christian sympathies. They too were burned.

During these persecutions it was common to go along a street calling people out of their houses according to a prepared list and to put out search parties for those who did not answer the call. When the roll-call was completed, everyone was taken to the Temple and ordered to make the pagan sacrifice. Those who did not were immediately executed. Such persecutions as these not only did not succeed in stamping out Christianity, but created a cult of martyrs and caused its more rapid growth.

Diocletian and Marcus Aurelius took on the Mantle of Divinity along with the Mantle of State. People in their presence were to prostrate themselves before them, as if in the presence of a God. This was not necessarily for reasons of personal vanity, but more to steady the ship of state and increase the authority of the Imperial court. There was a great concern at the number of soldiers who had taken the Christian faith, so the command went out to all legionnaires that soldiers were to participate in pagan sacrifices and swear an oath that they would fight against anyone they were ordered to, including Christians. Those who refused to obey this order were slaughtered. According to a record of St Maurice, a whole Legion was executed at Augorra. The Legionaries, who were themselves Christians refused to order their men to make the sacrifice. Twice the Legion was decimated, each tenth soldier being put to the sword. Finally, the entire Legion was slaughtered.

Despite widespread persecutions under Septimus Severus, Maximinian and Decius Valarian, the Christian religion continued to rapidly increase in numbers. The famed Roman writer Tertullian, coined the aphorism: "The Blood of the Martyrs was the Seed of the New Christians."

As time went on, there was little sign of the Christians weakening in their resolve, and even the pagans in the Roman populace became heartily sickened by the continual slaughter.

It became common to commute death sentences to forced labour in the mines. This at least stopped the wave of wholesale slaughter. But the sentence of forced labour was hardly a reprieve. More likely, it might best be thought of as extending the martyrdom to months and years. The mines were copper mines in Palestine, on the banks of the Dead Sea, or marble quarries at Sirmiun in Pannonia. The life in the mines or quarries was one of bestial severity. Christians sentenced were mutilated in a variety of ways. The tendon of their left foot was normally cauterised, so that any escape attempt would be impeded. The right eye was normally cut out with a knife and the wound burned with a hot iron. Young prisoners would normally be castrated. They were trudged across the desert under the burning sun. If they were married, their wife and children would go with them, even those of tender age. It was an extremely arduous journey. Many were like human skeletons by the time they arrived, many fell by the wayside and were left to feed the jackals.

Into this milieu of draconian persecution came Constantine.

Chapter 5
CONSTANTINE: THE FIRST CHRISTIAN EMPEROR

Constantine, to become known with historical hindsight as Constantine the Great, was born around 286, son of Flavius Valerius Constantinius, who was then the Cæsar or Deputy Emperor. In the hierarchy of Imperial Rome, there was one Supreme Emperor, but also there were several other rulers, who might be regarded as Emperor, roles that were often duplicated in both the Eastern and Western territories. The Augustus was the head of state and the Cæsar was his deputy. Constantine was brought up in the Eastern Empire, in the court of Diocletian at Nicodemia (in what is now Turkey). He grew up through all the horrors of Christian persecution, but was always thought to have had leanings towards Christianity. Through a series of political and military machinations, involving Galerius, Severus Septimus, Maximinus and his father, Constantinius, who by this time was Augustus, Constantine himself became a Cæsar, probably while still in his late teens or early twenties.

When his father died, in 306, the Roman army popularly acclaimed Constantine as Emperor. This was contested by Maxentius, son of Maximinus, Emperor of the Western territories. They became embroiled in a long series of complex civil wars, lasting over six years. In 313, the forces of Constantine finally invaded Italy and he won a decisive battle at Milvian Bridge, near Rome, where he defeated Maxentius. It is recorded that he had a vision, in which he received instructions for the battle from the Christian God. By one account, he was told to paint a particular Christian symbol, a monogram, onto the shields of his soldiers, or according to Eusebius of Cæsarea, he saw the symbol in the sky. Either way, the message was clear to him: "In this sign, conquer." This was his expressed inspiration for the spectacular victory.

Licinius, was the newly appointed ruler of the Eastern territory, in a deal forced on Constantine, following the death of Galerius, by the dead Emperor's supporters, who still had considerable political power. There was political and military tension between the two Emperors. In 324, Constantine defeated Licinius, at Adrianipole, and became the sole and absolute Emperor of all the Roman territories. Again, Constantine claimed divine intervention in the pursuit of this conquest. It was not unusual for military leaders to seek divine help in the course of military and political tribulations. Often Emperors would consult oracles or soothsayers for specific advice. What is remarkable is the vigorous way that Constantine developed after his conversion to Christianity: he set about a busy programme of rebuilding most of the churches that had been destroyed during the persecutions.

Under Constantine, we also have the first stages of the Christian Church moving towards an orthodoxy. In a series of letters, extending from 313 through to 320, Constantine postulated the implications of a schism that had begun to appear in the Christian Church. The Donatists, in the North African provinces, maintained that those Priests and Bishops who had lapsed during the persecutions, should not be allowed back into the Church. Constantine was concerned that a divided Church would offend the Christian God and bring about Divine vengeance upon the Roman Empire. He pointed out that schism was "insane, futile madness," but the Donatists countered that many had remained true to the Faith, despite awesome horrors that had been perpetrated against them during the persecutions. The ones who had given up easily and renounced their Faith, were not to be considered worthy to be readmitted into the Church. Constantine espoused that such a defiance of the intent of clemency in Christ's teachings, was a betrayal of Faith, which might incur eternal damnation at the Last Judgement. It was right for members of the Christian Church to show patience and long-suffering, for in doing so, they would be imitating Christ. Such patience would be Divinely rewarded.

No sooner had Constantine sorted out that little problem, than another, and perhaps more important schism began to manifest itself - the Arian controversy - probably the most important and significant doctrine to be called 'heretic'. Arius was born in Libya in 250 and became a Christian priest in the Egyptian city of Alexandria. He was a hugely successful preacher, attracting a large following through a message integrating Neoplatonism, which accentuated the absolute oneness of the Divinity as the highest perfection, with a literal, rationalist approach to the New Testament texts. Arius studied the concept of the Trinity and from this defined his doctrine of the Father as the One True God, the Logos (Word, or Son) being the most perfect among creatures and the Holy Spirit being the first creature of Logos. Jesus Christ was not God "made man," but God's first creature Logos, "enfleshed." Arius took, in the strictest sense, the message in the Gospel: "And the Word became flesh."

It is hard for us to imagine, from our modern viewpoint, how popular theological dispute could be, amongst the common populace. Theological argument was one of the prime forms of entertainment, stirring passions and discussions in everyday life. Not that people really understood the full implications of their discussions, but it is just like people today, when they meet socially, often speak about sport and politics, even though they know little about the first and nothing about the latter. Charismatic preachers were the real stars of their day. Arius was one of the most popular, with his reputation and his theological doctrine spreading far beyond his Alexandrian base.

Constantine's way of dealing with the problematic doctrine of Arius, would soon lead to one of the most important events in the history of Christianity - the Council of Nicæa.

Before examining more fully the debate that led up to the Council of Nicæa, some more pieces of the jigsaw need to be uncovered. It will be easier to understand the dialogue between Arius and the more orthodox Christian theologists, if we first look at what lay behind Arius' thinking - the theology of the early Gnostics and the doctrines of Mani, the Iranian prophet, whose name was to become synonymous with heresy.

Chapter 6
GNOSTICISM AND MANICHÆISM

The Founding Fathers of the Christian Church were specific and precise in defining the tenets of the new religion. The message of Jesus was clear for them and they evangelised with great enthusiasm. In one respect, however, they were a little woolly in their thinking. Concentrating their attention on the redemption from original sin as the Salvation for which Jesus had died, they somewhat ignored the problem of original sin. Yet they knew about sin. Living in a world largely at the mercy of the Roman Empire, they knew about sin all right. They lived a world of contemptible wickedness. But who was responsible for such wickedness? If God was the Creator and God was Good, why did he allow such evil to exist? And did he create such evil? They could recount the story of the Fall from the Bible, but that fell short of an explanation. The Fall could explain why man was encased in sin, but the Fall could not have created sin. More likely it was sin that had created the Fall. It was this question of the origin of sin that gave birth to the theology of Gnosticism.

The term Gnosticism is derived from the Greek word **gnostikos** - knowledge or one who knows. What he knows is **sophia** - wisdom - and **episteme** - knowledge acquired by learning or by empirical observation. Gnostic knowledge may therefore be different from other forms of knowledge, being derived not from ordinary sources, but from higher planes, from special divine revelations. Members of Gnostic sects believed there is a divine spark in human beings that comes from above and has fallen into this world, being subjected to fate, birth and death. It can be reintegrated into the spiritual world by a divine revelation. It has it obvious antecedents in Platonic philosophy and in the Jewish-Christian religion. There can also be traces of proto-Gnostic thought in the philosophies of religious thinkers, in Egypt, Mesopotamia, Iran, India or even early Greece. The followers of Plato and Pythagoras can be thought to have had a proto-Gnostic view. Gnosticism has its roots in Iranian Dualism, filtered through aspects of Judaism and Hellenistic thought. It is based on a concept of a Good God who is Absolute and Supreme Lord of all the Heavens, and a lesser God, a God of the Material World, who created everything tangible, including that which is evil. It arose and flourished in the Greco-Roman world during the period when philosophers, particularly the Pythagoreans and the Platonists, were seeking to transcend diversity and contradiction, and to find a religious foundation for thought. The essence of Gnostic knowledge was concerned with the place of human beings in the Universe. Their Universe was conceived as vastly larger than the world as perceived through the senses, and was superior to it. The Universe was viewed as a series of concentric spheres, with the Earth at the centre. The spheres were identified by the circular orbits of the planets, each governed by a specific deity. Beyond were the thirty 'æons' or primary spiritual powers, each corresponding to the thirty days of the month. If the Supreme Unknown power above is perfect and good, why does anything as imperfect as evil exist? The most widespread view seems to be that the spiritual world came into existence out of unions between pairs of æons. The 30th æons, 'Sophia' - wisdom - produced, or at least her desire produced, an inferior or imperfect Demiurge, sometimes linked with Yahweh, the Jewish God of the Old Testament. This less than perfect creator made the World, or possibly the angels, who were to be found with him, made the World. Passages from the Old Testament were read out to show how this God was a jealous God, claiming to be the one and only God. The angels that he created and had around him had names like Michael, Raphael, Gabriel. Gnostics believed that Jesus was a man into whom the spiritual Christ had come from above. The Christ was produced in the spiritual world. He could, therefore, reveal the mysteries of spiritual cosmology and the Christ spirit was responsible for Jesus' miracles. Obviously the revelation of knowledge was what mattered. The Cross existed as a symbol of the dividing line between the spiritual world and the what lies below. When Jesus was described as crucified, his crucifixion was simply the occasion for his ascension, when the divine spark returned to Heaven, and not as in Christian thought, as a sacrifice. Gnostic writings take the form of apocryphal gospels, letters, acts and apocalypses. There are links with Zoroastrian doctrine. The Apochryphon of John supposedly based on a revelation received by John, son of Zebedee, reinterprets the first few chapters of Genesis, saying the truth is "not as Moses said." Mostly, Gnostics rejected conventional worship, including prayer, fasting and almsgiving. True redemption was given to the inner spiritual man through Gnosis, while others held that a right called redemption was important and necessary. Redemption was intended to aid the divine spark in its ascent, following the death of the body, to the divine realms above.

It is difficult to disentangle relations between early Christianity and Gnosticism. The chronology is rather difficult and obscure. It is hard to differentiate causes from effects. Two main views have been held: that Gnosticism predated Christianity and influenced such Christians as Paul and John, even though they argued against it; or, that Gnosticism was a form of Jewish heterodoxy or Christian deviation or both. Probably not known to the New Testament writers, but flourishing from the early second century onwards.

There could be a third view: that the origins of the Gnostic and the Christian movements were virtually simultaneous, and that the story is therefore one of cross-fertilisation. It would appear that neither the Church fathers, nor the writers of the Gnostic Gospels could provide enough evidence for a decision to be made.

The fact that major Gnostic teachers claimed to have been taught by the disciples of Jesus proves no more than that second century Gnosticism was in contact with Christianity and probably owes much to it. Equally, in developing its organisational and doctrinal structures, the Church owes much to the Gnostics.

The Gnostic view of the Good God and the Lesser God is more commonly known as the Dualistic belief. The two most prominent advocates of this belief, Mani and Arius were born within forty years of each other, in the third century. Mani was born in Southern Babylonia, which was then part of the Persian Empire, but is now Iraq. He lived his early life amongst a Judaic-Christian sect, where for twenty-one years he formed his doctrines and nourished his vocational calling. Legend has it that he received visits and messages from an angelic source and that these annunciations propelled him to manifest his ideas and proclaim his doctrine to all. Mani's mission showed little sign of success initially, but within a few years, probably by around 242, Mani had permission from the King of Persia, Shapur, to preach his new religion throughout the Persian Empire. In doing this he would have the royal blessing and the protection of the local authorities. Mani travelled extensively, through the Empire, into India, Egypt and Khorasan. He had intended to found a truly ecumenical religion, integrating many of the teachings of other religious leaders, particularly Zoroaster, Buddha and Jesus. This was not to be a collection of religious bits and bobs, cobbled together in a more or less coherent fashion, but he drew from a variety of sources in an attempt to promote a truth that was capable of being equally translated into diverse formulas according to the different circumstances where it would be spread . The Indian, the Iranian or the Christian elements are there by varying degrees, revealed in Manichæan documents as components of an overall system that in reality was a particularly interesting form of Gnosticism.

Like the Gnostics, Mani postulated salvation through a special knowledge of spiritual truth. In fact it is more or less certain that Mani was influenced by the teachings of the Gnostics, Marcion, thought to have been the founder of the first dualist Christian church, and Bardaisan, more a philosopher than a religious leader. From Marcion, Mani took ideas about the organisation of a church, with two distinct classes of initiates and ordinary believers, or as Mani called the, Elect and Hearers. The Elect had passed through a strict ceremony and period of initiation. Such a process was open to men and women, but was only to be undertaken devoutly, for as a result of this initiation the Elect becomes full of Light and must, therefore, do nothing that would mingle the Light with earthy things. No Manichæan should eat meat, or drink wine, or marry, or hold property, or help in agriculture, or break bread. They were ordained to a wandering life, possessing only food for the day and clothes for the year.

More generally, the church that Mani established borrowed a good part of the apocryphal literature more usually associated with the Gnostic sects. Much of this was lost or destroyed over the centuries, but much was also rediscovered in 1945, in Upper Egypt, on papyrus scrolls sealed in earthenware jars. Some of this material has recently been published and is known as the Nag Hammadi Codices. Study of this material has strengthened the feeling that there was a link between Mani's teaching and those of the Gnostics.

Mani wrote down many of his revelations with his own hand and many copies were made by scribes. On the basis of comparative material, found in Egypt and in China, it has been determined that the Manichæan canon probably included at least seven works directly attributed to Mani himself. These are known as: 'The Living Gospel', 'The Treasure of Life', 'The Book of Secrets', 'The Pragmatia (or Treatise)', 'The Book of Giants', 'The Epistles', and

'The Book of Psalms and Prayers'. Two other works: 'The Drawing of the Two Great Principles', discovered in China, and 'The Principle Points of the Teaching of the Master', dug up at al Fayyum in Egypt, are believed to be recordings, by followers of Mani, of their teacher's actual words. Mani's teachings view man as being thrown into an alien, unbearable and radically evil world. He is enslaved in his body, in time and space, but desires to be delivered from this enslavement. If he is capable of experiencing this need for deliverance, it is because he is essentially superior to his present condition. God is nothing other than Goodness and Truth. He cannot have willed the suffering and deceit so characteristic of this world. Thus man's condition is attributable not to God, but to some other principle. The Soul of Man shares in the very nature of God. Souls are nothing other than a part of God that has fallen to Earth and is entrapped in the body. The interior illumination, or Gnosis, communicates to man what will help him know where he is, what he is, where he comes from, why he has fallen and where is he going. This Gnosis is expressed in a mythical form, and the unfolding of this myth is divided into three phases:

> a past period, in which there was a moment of separation, and thus a perfect duality of the two radically separate substances, Spirit and Matter, Good and Evil, Light and Darkness;

> a middle moment, corresponding to the present, during which a mixture of the two substances begins and continues;

> and a later moment, in the future, in which the primordial division would be re-established.

To accept Manichæism is to accept nothing more than this double doctrine, of the Two Principles and the Three Moments.

In the beginning there were two antagonistic substances, the one Absolutely Good, the other Radically Evil. Both were uncreated and eternal. Each one lived in a separate region, the Kingdom of God in the North, the East and the West, the Kingdom of Evil in the South. The Kingdom of God had, as its head, the Father of Greatness and the Kingdom of Evil had the Prince of Darkness. The former consisted of five dwellings, or members, of God: Understanding, Reason, Thought, Reflection, Will; and was inhabited by innumerable 'æons'. The latter consisted of five pits, one on top of the other, the World of Smoke, Consuming Fire, Destructive Wind, Slime, and Darkness, over which presided five Chiefs, or Archons, in monstrous demoniac forms, and where five different types of infernal creature swarmed about. Here, all was disorder, stupidity, abomination and stench, whereas the Kingdom of God was characterised by peace, understanding, purity and sweetness.

The middle moment opened with catastrophe. Darkness attempted to invade the Kingdom of Light. God decided to combat the danger by means of his own Soul, personified in his own Son, whom he evoked from himself, through the mediation of the Mother of Life. The Son was Primal Man. With his five sons, the five light elements, Air, Wind, Light, Water and Fire, as his armour, the Primal Man went down into the Infernal Abyss and his sons were devoured and swallowed up by the demons. Thus one portion of the substance of Light was mixed with, and enslaved to, the substance of Matter. From that point on God would devote himself to separating and freeing the Divine substance. With the exception of those who practice absolute celibacy, the shameful and painful successive imprisonment in bodily darkness, that has been forced upon the luminous Souls, will cease only at the End of Time, at the eve of the third movement of the myth. Then, after a period of apocalyptic calamities and the Final Judgement, the terrestrial globe will burn for 1,468 years. The lost particles of Light that can be saved will rise to the sky. The visible world will be annihilated. And Matter, with its demons, will be imprisoned within an immense pit, the absolute separation of Light and Darkness will be re-established.

The result of this cosmology is that man shares in the Divine Nature in virtue of his **nous**, his living self-consciousness. Salvation consists of him gaining consciousness of himself and of his relationship with God. This is accomplished by **gnosis**, in a particular manner, by the revelation of Mani and his church. At death, the man or woman might return to the original paradise of Light, unless persisting to keep the Soul in the impurity of the flesh and enslavery to material lustings. In such instance, the human will be condemned to rebirth, in a succession of worldly bodies. Thus, no fornication, no procreation, no possessions, no cultivating or harvesting, no killing, no eating of meat or drinking of wine, for those are contaminations of the Self, defilements of the imprisoned Light.

Mani built up a community of followers, during his mission, but also attracted the attention of many people hostile to his beliefs, particularly those representing the official orthodox religion of the Persian Empire, Sasanid, a form of Zoroastrianism, who were particularly intolerant of deviations of any foreign cults.

On the death of King Shapur, his son, Hormizd, succeeded him on the Persian throne and he soon yielded to the increasing pressure of the Magi, the leaders of the Sasanid religion, in cracking down on Mani and his growing legion of followers. The year was 276, and Mani was arrested. He was ordered to appear before the new King and the Magi. He was tested, tried, condemned, and thrown into prison. There followed twenty-six days of dramatic trials, to become later known as 'The Passion of the Illuminator', culminating in Mani being subjected to a form of crucifixion. Unlike the crucifixion of Christ, on the cross, Mani was cruelly chained up and allowed to gradually starve, weaken and die. Before he died, he summoned up a final burst of courage and strength to send a message to his followers, which he committed to several disciples attending to him. From this, it seems Mani viewed himself as the final successor of a long line of Heavenly Messengers, or Prophets, that had been sent to mankind, starting with Adam, and the principal ones being Zoroaster, Buddha and Jesus.

Mani had always been careful to call himself the Apostle of Jesus Christ, but felt that his particular interpretation of the message had universal meaning and value, and that it was destined to supplant all others before the End of Time. The Manichæan Church was thus dedicated from the beginning to a missionary ideal. Its permanent duty was to preach and to convert the universe. Whilst not quite achieving this, Manichæism did have its conquests, and from the third to the fifteenth centuries, echoes of it could be detected in large portions of the globe, from the European shores of the Atlantic to the Asian outposts of the Pacific. There were times when Manichæism had a more solid footing than Christianity and could even have supplanted it as a world religion. We will see later, that the orthodox Christians became so paranoid about the Manichæes, that the very word 'Manichæism' came to be used as a general description of all heretics and heresies.

Chapter 7
ARIANISM AND THE COUNCIL OF NICÆA

Whilst Mani was being crucified for his beliefs in the South of Persia, another dualist Christian prophet was establishing a following and a theological community of his own in the area around the Egyptian city of Alexandria, on the Nile delta. Arius, had been born in Libya in 250, his message, derived from an intensive study of the Trinity, accentuated the Absolute Oneness of the Divinity, with a rational reading of the New Testament texts. Christ was viewed as the most perfect creature in the material world, whose moral integrity led him to be adopted by God as a son, but who was a lesser deity - 'Logos' ('The Word' or 'Sun') - substantially unlike the uncreated, eternal Father and subordinate to his will. The Father is truly God, he is the only God and, being eternal, had not become, nor had he been generated . The 'Logos' is only a creature, but is the most perfect amongst all the creatures. The Father created him from nothing and proceeded through him to the creation of inferior beings. 'Logos', therefore, is not truly a God, but a Demiurge, an intermediary between God and inferior creatures. There was a 'when' when the Logos did not exist. But he is described by Arius as being, 'without Time' and 'before the Ages'. Vaguely, one can give him the title of God, because he is both a mediator between God and all his creatures and because God adopted him as his Son. He is, however, a Son by Grace and not by Nature. By his will he is determined to be Good, but of himself he is free and able to change. Not even the Holy Spirit is God. He is the first creature of the Logos and less noble. Thus the Trinity - the Father, the Logos and the Holy Spirit - in a perfectly balanced relationship.

Arius was not the first to dissent. Paul of Samosata, for example, whose teachings had been explicitly condemned by the church. But the philosophies of these predecessors had always been presented as the private opinions of a certain school of thought, without any intention of asserting them as the official doctrine of the church. They were attempting a philosophical interpretation of dogma. Arius, on the other hand, gave out his system as the official teaching of his church. He founded his doctrine, or thought he did, on the Gospels. It was already the practice of the church that private opinion was always subordinate to the official teaching - **sensus ecclesiæ**. But Arius was an expert on propaganda. He had a striking physical appearance. He was distinguished looking, in his advanced years. He was very tall, with drawn features, and a grave, pensive manner. He dressed in the style of the philosopher and the ascete, wearing a short tunic with sleeves and a cloak over it. He was gentle in manner, easy in speech, persuasive in argument, obstinate in opinion. He possessed great learning, even in profane matters and his morals were excellent. His thesis was publicised through the poetic verse and vulgate prose of his major work - 'Thalia' ('Banquet') - certainly the most efficacious method of propaganda amongst the working classes. His work was widely spread, mostly by way of popular songs, performed in taverns and market squares, for peasants, labourers and travellers It became a theology of the guitar, the poetic repertoire of sailors, millers and other working people. Such popularising of theological argument caused great consternation amongst the orthodox clergy.

There followed a series of heated debates, exchanges and condemnations between the followers of Arius and orthodox Christian clergy, in Egypt, Palestine and Syria, around the period of 323-324. Pamphlets of accusations and insults crossed each other in all directions. Synods were held by both sides and excommunications and counter-excommunications flashed across the Eastern sky. Everything was in disorder. Emperor Constantine, now the only Augustus, and the absolute ruler of the Empire, was anxious to maintain a modicum of unity and peace within his newly Christianised Roman Empire, sent emissaries to mediate in the theological conflict. These initial efforts failed and he summoned the first ecumenical Council of Nicæa, in what is now Iznik in Turkey, in May 325, to settle what he then termed "a fight over trifling and foolish verbal differences."

History was at a cross-roads. The Christian Church was about to confer orthodoxy on itself and as a consequence, heresy was about to be fingered.

When Constantine arrived at Nicodemia, near Nicæa, he was informed of the minute details of the new religious controversy. For Constantine, converted to Christianity without having fully embraced it, the dispute was about "small and vastly unimportant matters." Given that all Christians agreed that they should believe in one Supreme God, the Saviour of all, surely that is enough, without having to bother about questions that are beyond the intellectual grasp of most ordinary folks. Constantine's view was to let each one think what he wishes, but without losing concord and mutual respect for the theological views of others: "Give back to me, therefore, calm days and nights without worry; in this way, I also may have pleasure in the pure light and pleasure in a tranquil life for my remaining years." The words display his deep anxiety for public peace and unity amongst his clergy.

However, more aggressive theologians could not see that this was a 'small and unimportant matter'. This 'useless contest of words' was concerned with whether Jesus Christ, the founder of Christianity, was true God, or simply a creature. For them, it was a fundamental argument, a question of right or wrong.

None of the historians of the time, in relating the preparations for Council of Nicæa, ever mentions the Bishop of Rome, though other contemporary records show him as Pope Sylvester. It seems that Emperor Constantine was acting in the role of a sort of secular 'bishop', not because he considered himself head of the church, but because of his usual preoccupation in keeping peace within his lands. Constantine regarded this conflict within the church a gravely serious matter and Bishops were summoned from the remotest parts of the Empire. For general convenience, the city of Nicæa had been chosen, which was also close to Nicodemia, one of Constantine's seats of government. Historical accounts vary, as to how many Bishops attended the Council, but the number is assumed to be three hundred and eighteen. In fact, the Council of Nicæa came to be known, by later writers, as the meeting of 'the 318 Fathers'. There were representatives from the whole of Asia Minor, from Palestine, Phoenicia and Syria, from Egypt, Persia and the Balkans, from the Caucasus, Greater Armenia and Carthage in Roman Africa, from Spain, Gaul, Pannonia, and from Italy, with representatives from Calabria and from Rome itself.

The Council of Nicæa was a truly solemn assembly, not only because of the size, but also because of the dignity of many of the Bishops. Many of those attending still bore the scars of torment, undergone during the Great Persecution. There was Hosius, the Egyptian Bishop, whose right eye had been torn out and the tendon of his left heel cut, when he had been condemned to the mines. So great was Constantine's veneration for him that he was moved to kiss the empty socket of the eye, each time they met. Other members of the clergy, who had been crippled for their faith, were the Bishop of Neocæsarea, on the Euphrates, who had been maimed by having both tendons of his hands burned with red hot irons, the Bishop of Heraclea, on the Nile, whipped, starved and tortured, the Bishop of Epiphania, in Cilicia, blinded and crippled, and many other Bishops who had suffered persecution.

Constantine made a great show of the affair, treating all the members of the Council with sincere deference and royal munificence. Besides its religious importance the Council had great political significance, for it would be seen to renew the 'catholic nationhood' of the Roman Empire, bringing the Church and State closer together.

Bishops had already met amongst themselves to select the arguments for these discussions, and perhaps to agree on procedure. In these preliminaries, Arius was interrogated, and his case was well versed. In the main meetings of the Council, the Emperor was careful to keep his mouth shut during theological argument. He was intelligent and understood that this was not his territory. Had he spoken, it would be interesting to know what he might have said, since he had already characterised the Arian question as an 'empty search', arising from:

> "small and empty disputes over words - not suited to the good sense of priests and prudent men."

But Arius was given his platform, and used it well, frankly expounding his system of the Trinity in a clear and lucid way. He also called many powerful patrons, to help and defend him; such as, Eusebius of Nicodemia, Paulinus of Tyre, the local Bishop of Nicæa and Eusebius of Cæsarea. During the proceedings, passages from his 'Thalia' were read. This reading of religious doctrines in popularised, vulgate prose and lyrical verse, aroused lively indignation, to say the least, in the greater part of the assembly. Many of those present covered their ears, lest they should hear what they regarded as 'sordid and vulgar blasphemy'. It was at this point that the fate of Arius and his doctrine were, to all intents and purposes, decided. This was particularly so, because Arius insisted that there was indeed a 'when' when the Logos had not existed and therefore could not truly be God. His doctrine was on this fundamental point proved heretical, since it contradicted what the official orthodox church had always taught, that Christ was of God and was God.

The defenders of Arius grouped themselves, more or less openly, around Eusebius of Nicodemia, and they brought a letter before the Council, a Confession of Faith, proposing it as a basis for discussion. However, most of those present condemned it as heretical, because it was attempting to defend the indefensible. The letter was ceremonially torn up in front of the assembly.

It became the firm intention of the Council, with forceful advocacy from an influential congregation of Bishops who had grouped themselves around Athanasius, a celebrated leader and theologian from Alexandria, to formulate the doctrine that Logos was God, the true Son of God. This doctrine was to be formulated by using the terms found in the Sacred Scriptures, which should then be acceptable to everyone. The Arians, however, in the face of the heretical accusations levelled against them, accepted the formulation, but added that from various passages of Scripture, it was also possible to prove that men were the sons of God, were created in the image of God. Thus, they could accept, in a larger metaphysical sense, the doctrine of the Logos, as taught by the orthodoxy, in a strict and ontological manner.

Eusebius of Cæsarea also spoke. He gave general support to the Arians, to their devout dedication to the Christian message, without being wholeheartedly committed to their separatist cause. He was anxious to find a middle way, to show himself as a peacemaker to the Emperor. He proposed, as a basis of discussion, the Baptismal Creed used in Cæsarea, which had come originally from Rome. The most important part of this Creed was the word 'consubstantial'. Paul of Samosata had earlier taught that Logos was of the same substance as God the Father, but was in a different modality. However, this doctrine had already been condemned as heretical, at the Synod of Antioch, in 269. In arguing the case at Nicæa, Eusebius pointed out that the word 'consubstantial' signifies, etymologically, that one 'essence' can be predicated of two distinct 'hypostases', combining human and divine natures. But in the case of the Divine Trinity, the meaning of the word 'essence' can be interpreted, according to the catholic tradition, as 'nature'. The Logos, therefore, was of the same 'nature' as the Father. In such a tradition, Logos was 'consubstantial' with the Father, in so far as he was of the same 'substance' or 'nature' as the Father, though not the same Personage.

Constantine, with the help of close theological advisers, imposed the word 'consubstantial' as a **conditio sine qua non** for the approbation of the Creed. This was a decisive intervention, not because he was proposing any new theological argument, but because he had the power behind him. Acting with the authority of the Emperor, he threatened to exile anyone who refused to sign the Creed, in the form approved by the Council, with the inclusion of the word 'consubstantial'. Ditherers, and those not so committed to the Arian cause, gave in, and the only dissidents were Arius, two Libyan Bishops and some priests of Alexandria, who were friends of Arius. All of these were immediately sent into exile. Eusebius of Nicodemia and Eusebius of Cæsarea were among those who were half-hearted signatories to the Creed.

The text of the Creed, according to Socrates, the most authoritative historian of the Council of Nicæa, reads:

> "We believe in one God only, the Father, Omnipotent maker of all things, visible and invisible. And in one Lord only, Jesus Christ, the Son of God, the only begotten of the Father, that is from the essence of the Father, God from God, Light from Light, true God from true God; begotten not made, consubstantial with the Father by whom were made all things, whether in Heaven or on the Earth. Who for us men and our salvation came down, was made flesh, became man, suffered, rose the third day, went up to Heaven and will come to judge the living and the dead; and in the Holy Spirit."

Condemnation of Arius and his followers was summed up as:

> "Those, then, who say that there was a **when** at which he did not exist; or that before he was begotten he did not exist; or that he was made from nothing or from another hypostasis, or essence, or that the son of God is a created being, changeable or variable; those the Catholic and Divine Apostolic Church condemns."

The Council went on to discuss other schisms, to discuss the date on which Easter was to be celebrated and the devising of twenty canons, related to church discipline. These were grouped in topical categories, around four matters: the remnants of old schisms and heresies; the results of the last persecution, under Licinius; discipline of the clergy; and questions of ecclesiastical jurisdiction. In all, the Council of Nicæa lasted for over a month and, on the occasion of the formal closure, Constantine gave a solemn banquet for the members of the Council. It was also the twentieth anniversary of his assumption of Imperial power. Constantine felt satisfied with the work of the Council. Arianism had been condemned and its author was in exile. All the Bishops of the Council, except for two, had rallied behind the Creed. Victory seemed complete. Shortly afterwards, when visiting Alexandria at the invitation of Athanasius, he announced that: "Every division and all discourse has been dispelled from the splendour of the truth, by the will of God." In reality, there had been a forced consent. Many had disagreed with the Nicene Creed, but did not feel able to challenge the authority of the Emperor. Eusebius of Nocodemia and Eusebius of Cæsarea were still, more or less, loyally favourable to Arius, and were convinced that the term 'consubstantial' was erroneous.

Chapter 8
CHRISTIAN ROME & CHRISTIAN ORTHODOXY

The lack of success of state suppression against Christians in the Roman Empire, was a deciding factor in its turning from the hitherto official policy of persecution, to making it the Imperial religion. Constantine recognised the political implications of the unity of the Christian Church, which had manifested itself victorious and brought about the end of the persecutions. Ironically, it was when the Church became more tolerated that it, itself, became more intolerant. The elevation of the Christian Church to the Imperial Church of Rome contributed decisively to the external unification and pressed towards the elimination of pluralism, replacing a multiplicity of creeds, from the different strands of the Church, to a uniform Imperial confession of faith - the Nicene Creed.

Medieval heretical leaders were later to point out that the Church became corrupted when it was transformed from a persecuted, suffering Church, in the first three centuries, into a conquering Imperial Church during the Constantinian era.

Life went on for Emperor Constantine in matters of state outside of church matters. As was pointed out above, the Council of Nicæa coincided almost exactly with the twentieth anniversary of Constantine's Imperial reign. He was still not free from political intrigues, as with all Roman leaders, it was part of the Emperor's life. In one such incident, he had to have his own wife, Fausta, and his stepson, Crispus, put to death, to avert a political crisis in the Eastern part of the Empire. Constantine's expressed Christianity also made him many enemies in Rome. His refusal to take part in a pagan procession, on a feast day, offended many Romans, and once more hostilities broke out. He began to feel uncomfortable and insecure in Rome. Following the earlier defeat of Licinius, he had then renamed Byzantium, calling it Constantinople. He set his sights on rebuilding the city on a grand scale, to return it to its former status as one of the world's most majestic cities.

The dedication of Constantinople took place in 330 and this newly built city effectively became the new capital of the Roman Empire. His rebuilding programme of churches continued apace. His mother went on a pilgrimage to the Holy Land and as a result of this Constantine ordered the building of a superb basilica on the recently discovered site of the Holy Sepulchre. He involved himself, practically and creatively, in the church rebuilding process, offering suggestions for design and decoration. He commissioned a new copies of the Bible, for the growing congregations. He composed a special prayer for soldiers. He issued numerous laws relating to Christian practice, abolishing the penalty of crucifixion and the practice of branding criminals - "The human face should not be disfigured, it is of divine beauty." He enjoyed the observance of Sundays and Saints days. He extended privileges to the clergy and ended some of the more offensive pagan practices.

Despite the undoubted importance of the Council of Nicæa, controversy still raged within the church. It seemed a matter of destiny, that whenever Constantine meddled in the affairs of the church, he invariably made things worse. After Nicæa, Arianism was only apparently put down and it continued to spread and to grow, notwithstanding the Imperial measures taken against it. In the two years after the Council, many letters were in circulation, written by Bishops who had signed the decisions of the Council, but now showed unhappiness and distaste for the concept of 'consubstantial'. In 328, Athanasius became Bishop of Alexandria, renewing his vow to champion the Nicene Creed and the other decrees made by the Council of 325. However, another grouping of Egyptian Bishops came out strongly in support of Arius, hoping one day for an amnesty for him. Another schism had manifest itself, and Egypt became a seething hotbed of theological discontents. Accusations flew in all direction, Athanasius accused of all manner of ecclesiastical false practices, Arius being held up as a prime example of heretical doctrine.

Arius had another supporter, at the Imperial court. Constantinia, the Emperor's sister, brought a priest, who was a secret follower of Arius, to counsel Constantine. He spoke favourably to the Emperor, showing Arius to be perfectly orthodox and pointing out that what really had happened was that Arius had been misrepresented and persecuted by jealous enemies. When Constantinia fell ill, she asked her brother, as a last consummation before she died, to save the Empire by ceasing to persecute the innocent and by recalling the exiled, clearly referring primarily to Arius and his followers. In 334, Constantine sent Arius a letter, asking him to present himself at court. Arius did so and made a wary profession of faith, which could easily have been interpreted either in the Arian or in the orthodox sense, but which certainly did not contain the word 'consubstantial'.

Constantine was content. He revoked his sentence of exile and ordered that Arius should be readmitted to his rank in the clergy. However, Bishop Athanasius refused to accept him, still professing him heretic, and the church was once more riven with controversy.

Another Council was set up, this time at Tyre. But the arguments and counter arguments had become so convoluted that there was little chance of resolving such entrenched, opposing ideologies. After the Council of Tyre, the Bishops were moving to Jerusalem, to consecrate a new basilica. On this occasion, the assembly of Bishops, despite objections of the followers of Athanasius, took the opportunity to absolve Arius from all censure and to restore him to his ecclesiastical position. A letter was sent to all churches, pointing out what had been decreed in Jerusalem, and ordering it to be recognised. It must have seemed to the members of the Tyre-Jerusalem Council that the old troubles were at last over. Arius had emerged from exile and was back in the fold. However, looked at impartially, it was obvious that they had solved nothing, merely having changed the lines of argument. Instead of the old theological question, as to whether Logos was consubstantial with the Father or not, the question now was who was pulling the wool over whose eyes? There was still a great deal of unease in the church, with opposing factions attempting to outshout each other.

Constantinople. The afternoon of a Saturday in 336. The following Sunday Arius was to be officially received back into the Church. During that afternoon, Arius was walking, with some friends, around the city, showing himself off before his triumphal investiture. At a certain point, he felt the needs of nature, and asked if there were conveniences near at hand. He was near to the great Forum of Constantine and was shown to a convenience at the back of the Forum. He went in, leaving a servant outside. After some time, shouting was heard from inside. The servant ran in. He found Arius stretched out on the ground. He was already dead, his bowels having been ripped from his body and were strewn around his corpse.

Arianism and Manichæism had established an ideological counter-culture to the dogma of orthodoxy. They were both devoutly Christian ideologues, but were branded heretic. In this, they established a tradition of radical Christian thinking that was to be influential for centuries ahead, and would certainly be most important in the future destiny of the Medieval heretics - Cathar and Bogomil.

Constantine was still Emperor. He had considerable military success in the period following his Christian conversion, with triumphs over the Franks, the Sumarians and the Goths. These military victories also demonstrated that, despite his Christian disposition, he was nonetheless totally brutal towards his enemies. His victories were notable for their savagery and brutality, the sort of brutality that had become only too characteristic of Roman law enforcement.

Constantine was a Christian, and espoused the Christian cause, for most of his life, but was only baptised on his deathbed, in the year 337. For Eusebius of Cæsarea, Constantine the Great's reign was regarded as the fulfilment of Divine Providence. Constantine himself would not have objected to being told that he had changed the course of history.

Chapter 9
INTO THE MIDDLE AGES

At the time of the death of Emperor Constantine, the Roman Empire was in good shape. It had firmly established roots in both the Eastern and the Western world. Christianity had taken a firm hold, the magnificent basilica church of St Peter having been built in Rome and the Byzantine splendour restored at Constantinople. But decline and fall was on the agenda during the next century, some warning shots coming relatively quickly. Within ten years of Constantine's demise, the Roman Empire was once more split into Eastern and Western provinces, with separate Imperial rulers, and even these territories were under constant threat from external barbaric forces, particularly Visigoths and Huns, who had already made inroads into Europe and Asia Minor.

Emperor Theodosius briefly reunited the Empire and made Christianity the official religion of the Romans and their dominions. He was to be the last ruler of a unified Empire. And within seventy years there would be no Roman Empire.

This fifth century was a time of great instability, with rampaging hoards, moving around the globe, occupying lands from those in them and from each other. The door was opening on the Middle Ages, also known as Medieval times. This first part of the Middle Ages, from the final fall of the Roman Empire in 476 to the ascendancy of Charlamagne in 800, was known at one time as the Dark Ages, though this term is now broadly rejected by historians, because of its implicitly negative value judgement, in favour of Early Middle Ages. This was a time marked by frequent warfare and the virtual disappearance of urban life. It is certainly a time that we know relatively little about, as a brief glance at an encyclopædia or a book such as 'Timetables of History' will quickly illustrate. It is a time of little advancement in civilisation, of intellectual darkness and much barbarity.

The history of this period was intertwined with an ongoing territorial conquests in most parts of the Eastern and Western world. At various times there were invasions into Europe and Asia Minor by a wide range of pagan marauders: Avars, Hsiung-nu and Huns from the Far East, Goths, Visigoths, Ostrogoths, Vandals and Slavs from the Middle East, Picts, Jutes, Angles, Saxons and Vikings from the Northern countries, Francs from the Rhineland

However, Christianity did remain a constant throughout this period. Certainly in the West, where even some of the invading cultures took on some of the vestiges of Roman institutions and traditions and were converted to the Christian religion, most notably the dynasty of Frankish kings, known as the Merovingians, under Clovis I. In the East, the Byzantine Empire The Roman church now took over the role of the old Roman Emperor. The Pope had become the head of a united Catholic Church.

By the end of the 6th century the concept of a united church in a united Empire had disintegrated and disrupted. There were constant disputes between Rome and Constantinople, over the primacy of the church's authority. There was a great deal of corruption amongst the clergy, particularly in churches of Gaul and Spain. Things appeared to be going very bad for Christianity, when the turning point came. The salvation of the Christian church came not from the orthodox tradition, but from the Nestorians, who had been banished, and from the Copts in Egypt and the Celts in Ireland. These three groups of non-conformist Christians helped to spread the religion widely, at a time when it was under the severest of pressure in its original Mediterranean homelands. In the long term, the Irish Celtic missionary work proved to be the most enduring. But to begin with the gains of the Eastern Christians were easily the most impressive. Whereas the Coptic missionaries from Egypt were most active in Ethiopia, the Nile Valley, and in the Nubian kingdoms. The Nestorian Christians spread right out into the Far East, to china, to India, down into the South of Arabia and into Siberia.

However, no single event in world history in this period was more significant than the rise of Islam. The historic mission of its founder Mohammed, who was born in around 570, helped to weld together the fragmented Arabian peoples, through the unifying force of a new monotheistic religion. The prophet's message, submission to the almighty power of God, initially aroused hostility and upset the Meccans, who regarded it a threat to their own local cult. In 622, they forced Mohammed to withdraw to Medina, and this marks, traditionally, the beginning of the Muslim era. In 630 he returned to Mecca in triumph. In the story of the great expansion that followed, it is difficult to distinguish between the forces released by the new religion and the vital energy of the Arab. It was a period marked by a great upsurge of energy amongst the Arabian peoples, fuelled by the thrust of the new religion. These initial advances were greatly assisted by the exhaustion of the Roman and Persian Empires, both riven by religious dissent and discontent. Islam and Arabic forces made great inroads into Asia Minor, and North Africa, moved through Libya, crossed the Straits of Gibraltar into Spain. They also made conquests in Armenia, Mesopotamia and the Byzantine Empire, Turkey, Sardinia, Sicily, Corsica and made some inroads into Frankish territories, until they were defeated, halted and pushed back at the battle of Poitiers, in 732.

Spiritual conquests of Islam are at least as impressive as its military conquests and it remained a major religious force, continuing to gain adherents. Initially it was not a proselytising religion, Mohammed himself showing great respect for both Judaism and Christianity, whose prophets, from Abraham to Jesus, he regarded as his precursors. Jews and Christians were to be left alone to pursue their own beliefs. This allowed the Nestorian Christians to expand alongside the new religion of Islam and to coexist.

Historically the community of Islam developed into world civilisation with remarkable rapidity, in less than a hundred years, in fact. It showed extraordinary adaptive powers, absorbing many disparate peoples into a single, coherent, cultural unit, stretching from Spain, to Central

Asia, to Northern India. By the time of the High Medieval period, from the eleventh century onwards, Islam was being spread by tribal groupings, only partially Islamized, which were more barbaric and less committed to the true tenets of the religion. Many of these groups were more intent on destroying the civilisations that they encountered than they were in spreading the message of Mohammed. Doesn't this sound familiar?

The prophet's original intention was probably to regard the Jewish and Christian religions as of equal civil status to that of the Muslims. In fact, the Charter of Medina, promulgated by Mohammed, declares the Jews to be "a community at par with Muslims." There is even an invitation in the Holy Qu'oran for Christians and Jews to co-operate on the basis of monotheism:

> "O People of the Book! Let us come together in a principle that is common between us, that we shall not worship anyone beside God, and we shall not associate anyone with him."

In its earliest manifestation, Islam absorbed a whole series of institutions, customs and laws from neighbouring civilisations. This process continued up and into the Medieval period. The concept of *jihad*, or Holy War, is firmly implanted in the Islamic thought, but the classic Islamic position is that the world is divided into three spheres: the zone of Islam, where all are of the Muslim faith; the zone of peace, where reside those nations with whom the Muslims hold views of religious tolerance and peace pacts; and the zone of war, the rest of the world, regarded as threatening and hostile. The religious tolerance, promulgated by Mohammed, was broken down by the persecution of both Sunni Muslims and Christians by the Egyptian caliph, al-Hakim, in the eleventh century, who destroyed the Church of the Holy Sepulchre in Jerusalem and proclaimed his own divinity, thereby setting off a backlash that would soon bring about the first of the Crusades, the Christian version of the *jihad*.

Thus, at the time when Catharism was about to make a profound impact on European history, and when Holy War was in the air, Omar Khayyam was composing his Ruba'iyat, El Cid was a national hero in Spain, the cleavage between the Roman and the Eastern churches had become permanent, Macbeth had been defeated by Malcolm and Siward at Dunsinane, polyphonic singing was replacing Gregorian Chant and the harp was becoming popular in European music, William conquered England, killing off the English King Harold with an arrow in the eye, the whole event being recorded on the Bayeaux Tapestry, the Catholic church prescribed the excommunication of married priests, the building of the Tower of London had begun, the first gondolas had appeared in Venice and the Venetians had negotiated a trade agreement with Byzantium, and there was an increasing interest in matters astronomical with the publication of Toledan's 'Positions of the Stars' and Walcher of Malvern's 'Notes on the Eclipses of the Moon'.

                                                    And a new millennium has only just begun.

On Medieval maps, Christians placed Jerusalem at the centre of the world

Chapter 10
HOLY WAR: THREE CRUSADES

There is a popular romantic notion about Crusades, of Richard the Lionheart, and all that. Images of knights in shining armour, with white shields bearing red crosses and mounted on sturdy steeds. Ivanhoe, Robin Hood, King Arthur and the Knights of the Round Table. The Lionheart is up there with all these folk heroes. His brave warrior knights fought the good fight for us, for England, Dickie and St George, as Shakespeare might have put it, had he been around then. Images of these knights are present in churches, in stained glass, or laying in dignified repose in stone on the top of a marbled tomb. Books are written about them. Films are made about them. They represented chivalry, nobility and sacrifice for the protection of our land, our monarchy, our heritage. The very word 'Crusade' is synonymous with a just and noble campaign. People now crusade on behalf of the poor and disadvantaged, or to put right a wrong. There is something about the word that conjures up vigorous righteousness.

Nothing could be further from the truth. Richard the Lionheart was not even English, but was a Cœur de Lion, through and through, not even able to speak our language. Legend has it that he was not even interested in England, excepting that it was part of his royal domain, the Angevin Empire, stretching from the North of Scotland to the Pyrénées. He lived in France, in Anjou, the heart of his empire. When he died, his body was disposed as he had earlier decreed: his brain to the Abbey of Charroux, his embalmed corpse to lie with his father, another 'English' king, Henry II, in the abbey church of Fontevrault, in Anjou, and his heart to be buried at Rouen, in Normandy. Nothing for England.

But he came back from the Holy Land and saved us from the wicked King John, and to make all Englishmen free from serfdom, it says so in all the Robin Hood stories. Not quite! He did come back from the Holy Land, but to save **his land** from the usurping John. In those days it was all about territory, you see. Who owned what. Sod the peasants. Richard Cœur de Lion was a land-owning despot, and he loved to fight. In fact, fighting was the thing he loved best. So when the opportunity came his way to lead the Third Crusade, he grabbed it with both hands.

Now if we can be so wrong about our heroic Richard the Lionheart, what about the Crusades. We have been led to believe that Crusades were fought to save the Holy Land, from the invading infidels, from monstrous Saracens, from evil heathens. The Christian world would not have survived without these Holy Crusades and we should be eternally grateful for the bravery and sacrifice of the Crusading knights.

The Crusades were in fact largely populated by uneducated, poor people, persuaded to leave their peasant communities to fight for a Christian cause that would, at the very least, lead to their salvation, and that of their families, and they could also pick up great riches, treasures even, from those they killed in God's name. That they would be walking some two thousand miles, often with their families tagging along, having to pillage and rob for their food along the way; that they would eventually resort to cannibalism and crimes of severe barbarity, far worse than anything their opponents ever did. This was not explained to them before they went. Far from the Crusades being chivalrous and just, the opposite was nearer the truth, they represented one of the most barbaric acts of human inhumanity in the history of the human race. And that is saying something.

The First Crusade had come about because Pope Urban II was worried about two things that might be politically threatening. Marauding Turks, he explained, from Turkestan in Central Asia, had captured substantial territories in the Middle East, seizing lands from the Byzantine Christian Empire and were camped near to Constantinople. And the Holy City of Jerusalem was also still in the hands of the Infidel. At that time, every map showed Jerusalem as the centre of the world. It was a place of Holy Pilgrimage. The Pope preached against the Turks, calling them "an accursed race," them having adopted the heathen beliefs of the Muslims, and he promised any who went on the Holy Crusade, freedom from any penalties, in this life or the next, for wrongdoings, however bad they may be. This was a fighting pilgrimage, and anyone who could fight was welcome. It mattered little whether they were lords or thieves or murderers. Participation in the Crusade gave the promise of eternal salvation, as opposed to the fires of damnation. This was war as penance, a devotion for salvation, sending the Infidels to Hell. Crusaders would either loot treasure or die glorious, all in God's name.

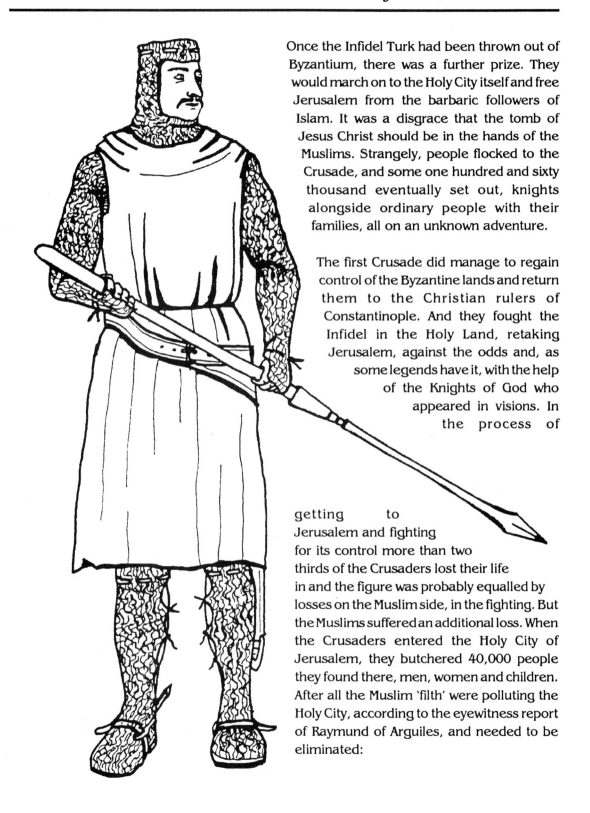

Once the Infidel Turk had been thrown out of Byzantium, there was a further prize. They would march on to the Holy City itself and free Jerusalem from the barbaric followers of Islam. It was a disgrace that the tomb of Jesus Christ should be in the hands of the Muslims. Strangely, people flocked to the Crusade, and some one hundred and sixty thousand eventually set out, knights alongside ordinary people with their families, all on an unknown adventure.

The first Crusade did manage to regain control of the Byzantine lands and return them to the Christian rulers of Constantinople. And they fought the Infidel in the Holy Land, retaking Jerusalem, against the odds and, as some legends have it, with the help of the Knights of God who appeared in visions. In the process of getting to Jerusalem and fighting for its control more than two thirds of the Crusaders lost their life in and the figure was probably equalled by losses on the Muslim side, in the fighting. But the Muslims suffered an additional loss. When the Crusaders entered the Holy City of Jerusalem, they butchered 40,000 people they found there, men, women and children. After all the Muslim 'filth' were polluting the Holy City, according to the eyewitness report of Raymund of Arguiles, and needed to be eliminated:

"Some of our men cut off the heads of our enemies; others shot them with arrows, so they fell from the towers; others tortured them, by casting them alive into the flames. Piles of heads, hands and feet were to be seen in the city. It was necessary to pick one's way over the bodies of men and horses. But this was nothing compared to what happened in the Temple of Solomon, a place where normally religious services are chanted. What did happen there? If I were to tell you it would exceed your powers of belief. Suffice to say this much, at least: that in the Temple and porch of Solomon, men rode that day in blood up to their knees and bridle reins. Indeed, it was a just and splendid judgement of God that this place should be filled with the blood of unbelievers since it had long suffered from their blasphemies."

One problem was, not all these people they massacred were Muslim. Some were Jews, and there were even some Christians. An inglorious sort of success. Huge losses and a reputation for savagery and butchery like no army ever had. The most brutal and bizarre story of all the horrors of the Crusade reputedly took place at Ma'arrat, fifty miles south of Antioch. Captured adults were cooked in large vats and children grilled on spits, to provide the Crusading army with a meal of human flesh. This sickening example of inhumanity was typical of the dishonourable way in which the campaigns of the Crusade were carried out. War as a penance, as devotion, for salvation.

The butchery and savage, bestial ways of the Crusade united the divided factions of Islam like no other act could, there was a general call to *jihad* and under Nur a-Din the stronghold of Edessa fell to the Muslims.

This caused even more antagonism in Europe. With all the loss of life on the first Crusade, now one of the conquests was back in the hands of the Infidel. They would be advancing on the Holy City itself next. Bernard of Clairvaux was rousing the crowds to once again take up arms and Pope Eugene III proclaims the Second Crusade in 1145, some fifty years after the first.

This one was an unmitigated disaster. The Muslim world was now united under one ruler Saladin and he proved to be more than a match for the invading Crusaders. There was great loss of life and Saladin even recaptured Jerusalem. But he did not slaughter the inhabitants, he even returned the sacred places for orthodox worship.

However, the Holy City was under Muslim domination and Holy War must raise its ugly head again. A leader was needed who would be a match for Saladin. And one was found in Richard the Lionheart. He raised a fortune for the Crusade, largely by imposing hefty taxes on the English peasantry that he could not abide. He took Acre, capturing thousands of prisoners. In a subsequent battle shortly afterwards, Saladin captured a similar number of crusaders.

When Richard realised that such a number of prisoners were something of a nuisance, holding him back from making advances, he took all four thousand of them outside the city walls and had them slaughtered. It took three days. No Muslims had ever treated Christians with such barbarity. In fact, Saladin released his prisoners, even after hearing what Richard had done to his people. There was something of a stalemate coming about. Richard and Saladin began to communicate and eventually came to a mutual agreement about the Holy City and freedom to worship there. A place of tolerance. This was enshrined in a treaty that both leaders signed. And Richard took his men home, getting himself captured in Austria, and held for ransom, which the poor people of England again had to pay.

One thing was sure, in all those years on the receiving end of persecution, the Christian Church had certainly learned how to persecute. The Crusades had not yet finished, but reflection on those first three gives the background to the story that was about to unfurl in Europe. The Crusades were largely about the pursuit of a certainty, that it was right to fight for the Christian cause. Like all other misguided certainties, they had been an expensive mistake. But that would not stop the Catholic Church proclaiming another Crusade, this time against Christians and within Europe itself. The Crusade against the Cathars.

CATHARS
and

CATHARISM

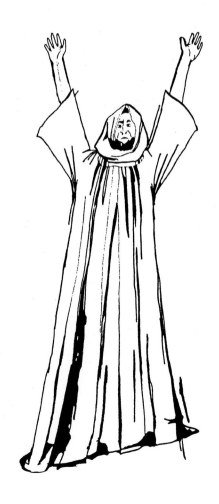

Chapter 11
IN THE LAND OF OC

Between the 10th and 13th centuries Languedoc developed and stood proud as the centre of a distinctive civilisation in the South of France. Broadly, the land of Occitania was taken to be the whole Southern region below the Loire Valley, an area that has commonly been known over the centuries as 'the Midi'. But the more specific region of the Languedoc was bounded by the Rhône in the East and in the West by Foix, the Pyrénées mountains to the South and the Auvergne to the North.

The Languedoc derived its name from the language spoken in this Southern region, langue d'Oc, or Occitan, in which the word '**oc**' means 'yes', as opposed to the Northerly way of saying 'yes' - '**oïl**' or '**oui**'. The language was spoken throughout the area, a distinctive language and a distinctive culture, which also embraced the romantic tradition of the **troubadours**.

The language and culture made a profound impact on the region and helped keep up morale during the years of invasion and persecution which were soon to come. The distinctive nature of this culture is still evident, even today, and there is a revival of interest in the language, with many books, poetry and other writings being currently translated into Occitan.   Since the 1930s, Joseph Delteil, René Nelli, Robert Lafont, Déodat Roché and Yves Rouquette have been key figures in maintaining the tradition in a contemporary world. There are an estimated 12 million Occitanian speakers, using dialects characteristic of Limousin, Auvergnat, Provence and Languedoc itself, little changed from those spoken in the Middle Ages. The Gascon language of Southwest France and the Catalan language of Northern Spain are also closely related to Occitan.

Languedoc was not a major power, but was one of the major centres of western culture. And the area was stoically independent. The langue d'Oc, the Occitanian tongue, was a language of literature par excellence, for many French, Italian and Catalan poets alike. Dante had originally intended to compose his Divine Comedy in Occitanian. As well as its celebrated links with Catharism, the region is still best remembered as the land of the troubadours. Troubadours, the inventive strolling minstrels, who attached themselves to the courts and noble houses, writing songs in the most complex of lyrical forms: songs of romance, songs of love. Troubadour verse deals not with love itself, but with the method of obtaining moral and spiritual perfection, with the help of love. Their songs gave a flavour to the region, to the age. Passionate, sincere and a little unreal. The noble families of the region embraced the spirit of the troubadours to their bosoms. This was a turbulent, restless, egotistical society, given to prodigal extravagance. They were obsessed with apparently impractical arts and were hungry for unattainable loves. The nobles of Languedoc were also sympathetic to the

Catharism that was gaining it popularity throughout their provinces. Not only were they sympathetic, but they became its most steadfast supporters. This was not just because the religion had won over a majority of their subjects, though this would have contributed to their acceptance, but Catharism had found favour amongst the women of noble families. Catharism was a religious doctrine that permeated, unlike more orthodox traditions, from the so-called lower classes upwards.

The Languedoc was Catholic, in theory and actuality, yet by a natural process, it had become, in the eyes of the established church, a land of heretics. By the year 1200, the population of the Languedoc region had turned its back on the extravagance of the Catholic church, but without any dramatic or overt rebellion. A certain proportion of the aristocracy remained faithful to Catholicism. The Papal legate, Pierre de Castlenau, had succeeded in forming a league of barons, for the purpose of combating 'heresy'. However, it seems that most barons only agreed to this action to upset the Count of Toulouse, rather than out of any great loyalty to the church.

The bishops considered themselves, after God and the Pope, the Country's rightful masters. They were feudal landlords, with vast territories at their disposal and considerable revenue. They looked after the spiritual needs of those who lived in their particular patch. The Catholic church in this region, at this time, had neither authority nor prestige. Catholics were reduced to either making do with a church that offered little leadership or seeking out some other outlet for their spiritual aspirations.

What the people saw was a powerful and corrupt church, involved in an extravagant accumulation of wealth, meddling in politics. There were bishops behaving badly. There were priests without the moral stature to engage the respect and allegiance of the population they were supposed to serve. The political situation was grossly unstable. Even in the eyes of Pope Innocent III, the clergy in this region had sunk to pitiful levels. He accused them of selling justice, damning the poor, and of giving absolution only to the rich. They did not even observe the laws of the church, being more concerned with acquiring personal benefits, entrusting the priesthood and other ecclesiastical responsibilities to unworthy pastors.

Consequently, God and his church were held in contempt. For Pope Innocent III, the prelates were a laughing stock of the laity throughout the region. They lacked any sort of moral or spiritual respectability. For example, Innocent III on Bérenger II, Bishop of Narbonne:

"This man knows no other God but money and keeps a purse where his heart should be. During the ten years that he has held office, he has not once visited his own diocese, never mind the province as a whole."

Innocent III pointed out that, regularly, monks and cannons had cast aside their monastic habits, had taken wives or mistresses, and were living by usury. Some indeed had set up as lawyers, jongleurs or doctors.

The political situation was very complicated in the area. There were lands under sovereignty of the French crown. There were lands, almost as extensive as those that owed allegiance to French crown, under the sovereignty of Count of Toulouse. The Count of Toulouse had many vassals, who ostensibly owed him allegiance. Primary amongst these were the counts of Montpellier, of Foix, and of Comminges, and the Viscount of Béziers. The Count of Toulouse was also sandwiched between two sovereigns. The King of France, to whom, in theory, he held allegiance, and the King of Aragon, the monarch who controlled certain areas in the heart of Languedoc, principally Montpellier, Carlat and Millau. The Count also had a part of his domains in fife to the King of England, Henry II. The kings of France, Aragon and England had all given the hands of their sisters in marriage, in return for the allegiance of the various counts of Toulouse. There was often disunity and disharmony amongst these powerful overlords. Nor was there any consistency of loyalties. For example, when the King of England, Henry II, was at war with Richard Cœur de Lion, his own son, Richard had taken upon himself to invade the Toulouse area, at the head of one of his mercenary armies, but later gave the hand of his sister, Joan, in marriage to Raymond VI, Count of Toulouse.

Towards the end of 1207, Raymond VI, the current Count of Toulouse, found himself at the centre of a political intrigue, inaugurated by the Papal legate, Pierre de Castlenau. Over a century before, his illustrious ancestor Raymond IV had given his life, in service to the Pope and the Holy Catholic church, at the forefront of the first Crusade to the Holy Land. Now the young Count of Toulouse was being asked to join a league of Southern barons in order to hunt down 'heretics' in his own lands. As one of his chevalier knights said, when asked why they did not break up the heretics and drive them out:

"We cannot do it, we were all brought up together, many of them are related to us, and besides, we can see for ourselves that they lived decent honourable lives."

Vassals of the Count, however, were more interested in protecting their own corner. The Viscount of Béziers, for example, had established possession of domains that included the districts of Carcassés, Albigeois and Razès. These lands, stretching from the Tarn to the Pyrénées, were in the further vassalage of the King of Aragon. Various vassal leagues were constantly being formed against the Count - formed and then dissolved, according to the state of each member's aims and interests. But this was the norm. Such political conditions prevailed in almost every Western kingdom. The kings of France were continually being forced to defend themselves against vassal leagues. In England there was a systematic fight against the royal prerogative, which culminated in the signing of the Magna Carta by King John. Germany and Italy were scenes of continual warfare.

In this political melting pot, with the church also in disarray, the Cathar church grew, flourished and prospered. The Cathars had many friends amongst the nobility and their supporters were certainly powerful enough to defend themselves. Even if he had wanted to, the Count of Toulouse did not command sufficient strength to provoke a civil war. Nor had he the will to do it.

The current Count of Toulouse, like his predecessors, was forever embroiled in disputes with bishops and vassals, though people continued to show him the greatest of respect. The burghers and the peasants were relatively free human beings, largely through the increasing opportunity and development of trade. Most humble artisans were gradually being transformed, developing into a relatively prosperous class, with full realisation of their rights. The orthodox Catholic church was seen as being corrupt and immoral. Consequently, what the Catholics defined as 'heresy', was the non-acceptance of an already defined, dogmatic Christian orthodoxy. 'Heresy' could be thought of as proliferating everywhere. There were remnants of supposed defeated creeds, Arian and Manichæan, which cropped up incessantly, sometimes in the shape of a compromise with orthodoxy, sometimes in direct opposition to it. The abuse that was characteristic of the established church, provoked a never-ending stream of protest and reform, which more often than not became regarded as 'heresy', merely by definition of their opposition. However, it was commonly regarded, by the church authorities, that in parts of the North of Italy and in the Languedoc, a very different state of affairs existed that was no longer a local matter of individual statements of independence, criticism or reform. What they saw happening in these regions, particularly in the Languedoc, constituted a rival religion, that had planted itself at the very root of Christendom.

For the church of Rome, these were no longer dissident Catholics, they drew their strength from the deep-seated consciousness of belonging to a strand of the Christian faith that had long been at variance with orthodox Catholicism, and with more ancient and authentic roots, even, than the church of Rome itself. They were the Cathars.

There were other reforming sects, regarded as 'heretical' by Rome, such as the Waldensians and the Lombards. Peter Valdes of Lyon preached from 1161 to 1180, his followers forming a numerous sect stretching from the Lyonnais across the Alps into Italy. Peter Valdes underwent a profound religious experience, that caused him to rid himself of his wealth and his family, to appear in the streets with urgent appeals to his fellow citizens to repent. More like Protestant Christians than adoptionists or dualists, as were the Paulicians and Cathars respectively, they were nevertheless categorised 'heretic' due to their ascetic anti-clericism. Another sect, of 'Lombards', said to have been organised by an Abbott from Italy, a rebellious reformer called Arnold of Brescia, was more loosely defined, emerging under a variety of names and guises. Thus, by 1184, a group called the 'Arnoldists', after their originator, was restating his teachings. They held that Catholic prelates and priests were entirely unworthy to represent the true church of Jesus Christ. For them, the test of a true Christian was the profession of poverty, the poverty of the apostles. They considered that even laymen, in this state, had every right to preach the Gospel.

In the North of Italy, it is most likely that 'heresy' took the form of Bogomilism, imported from the Balkans.

At times, all of these so-called 'heretical' sects were confused with the great 'central heresy' of Catharism. Cathars, the 'pure ones', with historical precedents that came most probably from the East. It was often labelled 'Manichæism', as there was a tendency to give this name to all such 'heretical' sects that appeared in Western Europe in the eleventh century and onwards. Various sects which were assumed to be 'heretical' never claimed any connection with Manichæism or acknowledged connections between themselves. After all, it was common knowledge that anything branded 'Manichæan' would be condemned with anathema and were burned on bonfires.

It was possible, however, to identify a link between the Bogomils and the Cathars, specifically, and to establish links with earlier dualist theologies.

The Cathars were first and foremost Christians, indeed they were very devout Christians. They had, perhaps, little in common with the Christianity associated with the thousand year development of Catholic orthodoxy. They had much in common with the Gnostic Christians, who in turn had strong doctrinal influences on the dualistic tradition of Mani and Arius. The Manichæans had spawned a series of powerful sects, spreading right across Europe and Asia, penetrating as far as China. At one time Manichæism had more followers than any other form of Christianity. But they had suffered a series of cruel persecutions and had ostensibly vanished. The name of Mani had virtually been obliterated by that of Christ, even though the former had firmly rooted his theology in the words and messages of Jesus the Christ. Orthodoxy had struck out and vanquished.

There had remained the remnants of a proselytising sect known as the Paulicians, a quasi-Manichæn sect that had strong Christianising tendencies, flourishing primarily in Armenia and Asia Minor. In 872 they had been suppressed by the Greeks, forced into submission, many of them being deported to the Balkan peninsular. It was here that they probably formed the nucleus of the church that was later to become closely associated with the Cathars. The Bulgars had settled in the Balkans in the seventh century and the deported Paulicians engaged in missionary activity amongst these settlers. By the tenth century a distinct sect known as the Bogomils had developed. It is not known for sure if the founder of the sect was called 'Bogomil', as some have suggested, and applied his name to the creed he had founded.

'Bogomil' means 'friend or beloved of God', so it may have been that, in accordance with a tendency common amongst the Slavs, the word was used to suggest some symbolical, generalised personality. In the latter case, devotees of the sect must ultimately have assumed the existence of a real flesh and blood founder, for there existed a profound belief in a man called Bogomil.

Bogomilism spread rapidly, and though its origins are shrouded in some obscurity there is no denying the dynamic force by which it spread throughout the whole Mediterranean world. It first gained ground in Bosnia and Serbia. By the eleventh century it was well established in Northern Italy and had encroached into the Languedoc, where it further transformed itself into the dualist tradition we know as Catharism.

In 1167, the Bulgarian Bishop, Nikita or Nicétas, arrived from Constantinople for the purpose of confirming the churches of the Languedoc to be of the true Bogomil tradition.   He called a council of Cathar bishops and ministers at St Félix-de-Caraman, near Toulouse. Evidence from contemporary written records demonstrates how far the Cathar church had gone towards proclaiming itself as a universal and self-evident organisation, in direct defiance of the church of Rome. At this point it was no longer merely a sect, in the eyes of the Catholic authorities in Rome, but had become a church of its own.

After the Cathar Council of St Félix-de-Caraman, the followers of Catharism made no attempt to hide themselves. Assured of popular support, even their leaders felt able to defy the authorities and the circumstances were ideal for nobles to join their ranks. In the South, nobles had long been jealous of the vast estates and the opulent possessions of the church, and the amount of political importance they were able to impose on the region. At one stroke, the nobles of the Languedoc were able to hit out at the abuse and excesses they saw in the church and to ensure the co-operation of their local Catharist populations. Catharism, despite its gnosis, was essentially a popular religion. Amongst the ranks of the Cathar followers would be cloth-merchants and doctors of medicine, two professions that regularly came into contact with the noble classes, and particularly the women in the noble classes. In this way, the Cathar faith gradually became part of the lifestyle of the nobility as well as the general population.

As far as the majority of people in the Languedoc were concerned, the adherents of Catharism were merely people who devoutly believed in Christ and worshipped him, as best they felt able, in their own way.

Chapter 12
CATHAR CULTURE AND RELIGIOUS RITUALS

a.   Cathars?

It has long been accepted that the word 'Cathar' comes from the Greek 'Katharos', meaning 'pure'. However, it is unlikely that the Cathars ever even referred to themselves as such. The term was more probably employed by adversaries and could even have been used in a pejorative sense. It has been suggested that the name may have come from the Latin 'catus', meaning of course 'cat', because it was said that they "....kissed the hindquarters of a cat" - the form in which "Lucifer appears to them." Like the "smell emerging from the backside of a cat." Such insults can be accounted for by the fact that the Cathars attributed creation of the material, visible world to a Principle of Evil, although their version of 'evil' simply meant anything less than 'Godly' and did not have all the trappings of Satanism and Diabolical Hellfire that the Catholics have heaped upon the word.

In Medieval traditions, notably in Germany, the cat was seen as symbolic of the Devil. In Medieval German the word 'ketter', meaning 'heretic' is closely related to 'katte', meaning 'cat'. Thus it was easy to spread the rumour that worshipped the Evil Creator in the form of a cat, where in actual fact, nothing could be further from the truth. This was a classic piece of Catholic disinformation.

Dualists were branded with numerous names. In Germany and in the Languedoc region of France, the were the Cathares. In Flanders they were called the Poplicain and Piphles, in Italy and Bosnia they were called Patarins and Bogomils, and in Northern France these became the Boulgres or the Bougres, a particularly derogatory form of expression that has since become synonymous with sodomy. This was no doubt another piece of Catholic disinformation, used to explain the Cathar celibacy. If they don't have sex with the opposite sex they must be homosexual.

Geographical terms were also used: 'Heretics from Agen, Toulouse, Albi....' In fact, this latter became 'Abligensian' and was almost as successful as the word 'Cathar' in describing adherents of the sect, even when used of people far away from the Albi district. Thus the persecution of the Cathars in the Languedoc became known as the Albigensian Crusade.

b.   Parfaits and Parfaites

The ministers of the Cathar church, the 'bishops and priests' of the Cathar faith, have become known as the Perfecti, or in the feminine equivalent, the Perfectæ. This name reflects the striving for goodness that was fundamental to the life of strict observance they had chosen. Names are difficult to tie down in relation to the Cathars, as most documentation was destroyed, either during the two Albigensian Crusades or in the subsequent Inquisition. The nomenclature that has come down through the ages may well be more related to names given to members of the sect, rather than names they gave themselves. Many scholars have made a case for believing that Cathar believers referred to their ministers 'Bons-Hommes' and 'Bonnes-Dames', a simple statement of the good men and good women that they tried to be. They were also known as the 'Friends of God', an expression no doubt directly relating to the Bogomils ('Bogomil' meaning 'Friend of God' in the Bulgarian). In fact, to be absolutely correct to the spirit of the times, given the Bogomils in the Balkans and the Cathars in the West, one should more accurately describe these dualist churches as the 'Church of the Friends of God'.

However, certain names have become accepted to describe the roles adopted by ministers and followers of the Cathar church. 'Perfecti' is now commonly taken as the name for the Cathar ministers, though a whole female group of ministers would be known as Perfectæ. The French versions of these commonly used are 'Parfaits' or 'Parfaites'. Whether these were names they chose for themselves, or whether they were given as a form of cynical abuse - 'those who call themselves perfect' as in the Inquisitional use of the term 'hereticus perfectus'- the words are now generally taken to describe those people who tried to live a life of perfection, in order to minister to the needs of their fellow beings, in this life, and to rejoin their God Almighty in the next.

In the main, I will mostly use the term 'Perfecti' to describe the Cathar ministers, but will occasionally use the terms 'Parfaits and Parfaites' or 'Bons-Hommes and Bonnes-Dames' to remind us that men an women were ordained to the Cathar ministry, and to avoid the dogmatic tendency of only using one piece of terminology.

The Perfecti were distinguishable by their grave, yet moderate utterances, by their habit of constant prayer and by their endless discourse concerning God. They gave up all their worldly possessions, lived a pure and sanctified life, and were always ready to give succour and to selflessly help those in need. They never shunned even the vilest outcast's company - a strange paradox in the case of people who so despised the material nature of the body - but this was a powerful tool by which to propagate their cause. A good doctor is given a particular sort of respect. The Cathar minister stood much closer to their flock than any Catholic priest. They were poor like the people and shared their labours. They were not above working at a loom or giving reapers a hand with the harvest. They gave courage to the poor through the example of their own lives, which indeed was harder than the poorest peasant. To their followers, they embodied a genuine sort of power and authority, with no need for excessive pomp or ceremony in order to impose their will. They were the church of love, offering violence to no one. Their church, consequently, flourished and grew prosperous, as those who converted to it could now feel that they were part of a community which offered a greater unity, a richer spiritual life and more inner sanctity than the Catholic church could ever offer.

Followers of the Cathar church were called credentes or believers. It is unlikely that the boroughs or County estates were composed wholly of Cathars, but it has been established that in many areas they formed a distinct majority. They were more numerous in some guilds than in others, for example, amongst, farm labourers, carpenters, hatters, tanners, saddlers, hawkers or, most commonly, weavers - in fact, 'weaver' was a popular nickname for any 'heretic'.

It is not easy to say precisely how the Catharist church was organised, as almost all of the Cathar church's own records and ecclesiastical documents were destroyed. There are documents remaining, but largely written by Catholic sources, such as comprehensive Inquisition records, like those, in particular, from the village from Montaillou, extensively recorded by the Inquisitor assigned to that village, Jacques Fournier. From such documents, and the few remaining Cathar texts, it is possible to build up a clearer picture of Cathar life. We do know that Cathar faith was well integrated into the daily life of many communities.

It is known that the Cathar church was organised. There is no evidence of there being an overall head, a 'Pope of the Heretics', though it has been suggested that Nicétas, the Bogomil leader from Constantinople might well have been seen in this role. This is unlikely. However, the Cathar church, in the Languedoc, and elsewhere, was organised into diocese. After Nicétas made his evangelical visit in 1167, presiding at the Cathar Council, held at St Félix-de-Caraman, four specific diocese were created: Albi, Toulouse, Carcassonne and Agen. A fifth was created in 1226, the diocese of Razès. There were others.

Each province had its own Bishop, together with two assistants, known as filius maior and filius minor; before he died the Bishop would ordain the filius maior as his successor. In turn the filius minor would become maior and a replacement minor would be chosen by congregation of Perfecti. Each important locality had its Deacon, assisted by a varying number of Perfecti, both men and women. There were never very many of these in each district, but it is known, for example, that there were over a thousand Perfecti recorded in the Languedoc alone during the period 1200 to 1250.

The ideal believer would live a life of perfect chastity, eat only a minimum of vegetarian food and deny any physical pleasure or comfort. The Cathars abstained from eating meat, because the meat might contain a segment of a refined soul, which would then become more earthbound, by a process of metabolism

Cathar authorities realised that a life of complete negation was beyond the reach of the average mortal, so they encouraged casual debauchery amongst their followers, as preferable to marriage, as marriage was more likely to lead to procreation, and the further imprisonment of souls.

There were no church buildings, no grand meeting places, no ostentatious temples. The Cathar meeting places were called 'Houses'. There would be an Elder or a Prior in charge of each House, which was both a workplace and a seminary. Novices were given a professional training as well as the moral and theological education that would eventually assist them to become Parfaits or Parfaites.

The Perfecti had an obligation to carry out manual labour, alongside the other Cathar believers in their constituency, but they also had a greater obligation to devote most of their time to prayer and to preaching. During this time they

would strive continuously to give clear and concise meaning to the New Testament, particularly the Gospel of St John and the Book of Revelation. Many would go from house to house, ministering to the needs of the people, and they would preach anywhere, in public squares, market places, in fields or orchards, and in private houses.

Every month the whole community would perform a rite of 'Service' or 'Apparelhament'. The Perfecti performed an act of submission and confessed before the visiting Deacon, with believers in attendance. A sermon followed and the whole ceremony ended with a Kiss of Peace. Thus the church kept in close contact with the mass of the faithful.

Cathar Perfecti went round in twos, as a minimum. They dressed in habits with large wide sleeves and hoods, black or dark blue, giving rise to the expression 'to take the habit' when referring to ordination. Males usually wore beards, though would have to shave these at times of severe persecution, so as not to be too distinguishable from the general population.

The Cathar Perfecti lived a life of austere asceticism, reminding us of the most rigorous of monastic traditions. But contrary to what happens in Catholicism, it was not only a disciplinary exercise, detaching oneself from the world in order to serve God better, but it had a metaphysical value. It found its justification in dualism itself. If God was absolute purity, then it made absolute sense for the followers of God to attempt to attain such purity. In order to attain such a level of purity, strenuous religious observances had to be made. Firstly, all meat or any food of animal origin, meat, fat, tripe, milk, eggs, butter, cheese, was strictly forbidden. There was in every animal a soul awaiting salvation and its destiny should not be interfered with. In fact all flesh came about through an act of generation which was, in essence, diabolical, the sense that all material things were diabolical. Strangely, it seems that fish, a reputedly 'cold-blooded' animal was allowed to be eaten.

Parfaits and Parfaites were obliged to undergo three periods of abstinence each year. The first of these was before Palm Sunday, the second after Whitsun, and the third before Christmas. Throughout the year they would fast on bread and water on Mondays, Wednesdays and Fridays.

Another absolute obligation was continence. This was not primarily a question of celibacy, or simple disciplinary chastity, but the act of generation itself was a procreation of material things. And material things were less than Godly things. The act of generation was seen as delaying the liberation of souls. Bodies were regarded as 'fleshly prisons'. The act of union between man and woman was seen as a process of creating more of these 'fleshly prisons'. Carnal union, therefore, was less than Godly and no sacrament could sanction it. The Catholic church consecrated sexual union by marriage and the Cathars, therefore, accused the Catholics of acting by proxy. The observance of this rule was so strict that a Parfait or a Parfait e was not allowed even to touch a member of the opposite sex, or even brushing against them in the process of everyday life.

c.   The role of women in Cathar society

CATHAR EGALITARIANISM - from 'Les Femmes Cathares' by Anne Brenon

It is up to us to bring to light with our everlasting human - or feminine -common sense the great or small reasons, practical, intellectual, secret, obvious, exaltingly, reassuring or weighty that motivated women of six to seven centuries ago to entrust their life and their hopes to Catharism. Indeed all those reasons could equally have been shared by men.

We have a nearly perfect knowledge of Catharism in so far as its theological education, its religious rites, its ecclesiastical organisation, its method of exegesis of the scriptures and even its sociology, at least in the Occitan culture. But what of the precise and tenuous link that connects to Catharism the will of all these apparently normal beings, normal women - and normal men, their men - what does this same sociology reveal?

The theoretical teaching of Catharism say that the souls of human beings, angels fallen from divine heaven and created by God, these souls are all 'good and equal' and that the Devil alone created a difference in the body. The body alone bears the stigma of inequality through sex. There are no specifically masculine or feminine souls:

"All souls are good and equal . . ."

Some are simply already awake whereas others, most of them, are still asleep and of course, in a marriage there was no way of proving that the husband's soul was any more developed than that of his spouse.

When a knight of good heretical belief happened upon a group of Good Christian women on his path, he would promptly dismount and deeply bow three times before them even if, previous to receiving the spiritual baptism, they were no more than simple peasant women.

The Cathar church, of course, did not sanctify marriage. It acknowledged this as a non-religious institution, and the families of the Cathar believers were based on the issue of one couple, just like in any other families. But the Cathar church steadfastly refused to recognise, in this profane act, a divine sacrament. In any case, the only sacrament that the Cathar church recognised was that of the baptism of the laying of hands (the Consolamentum). And it equally strenuously rejected all the arsenal of Roman sacraments, from that of Eucharist to that of penitence. Marriage, last born and latecomer to the sacraments instituted by the Papal church, could only have appeared to the Cathars as the one with the least foundation.

For marriage to be an agreement, of social and profane character, so be it, but it could under no circumstances represent a sacred bond in the world of the Good Men, between their believers, male and female. The act of the flesh for Good Christians was listed amongst the sins forbidden by the precepts of the Scriptures, in the same way as lying, theft, perjury or murder. Indeed, they took a vow to abstain from it. For ordinary believers, not yet free from evil, this was not an absolute interdiction. Certainly the sin of the flesh could not be pleasing to God - in so far as God would bother to observe the behaviour of humans in this world below - because it engages only the body, which is the evil and corruptible part of a being. But, conversely, this sin would appear more serious within marriage, if this action, alien to God, was sanctified. Maybe it appeared more mechanical and to have sprung from more murky impulses, than a disinterested act of love between free lovers. Marriage normalised the act of flesh, tying it to the legacy and material interests within families.

Free union, tolerated; marriage, desanctified; dilution of the notion of the sin of the flesh by diluting both adultery and conjugal duties; did Catharism represent, in fact, a breath of fresh air for the Medieval woman?

The Good Men, though they did not celebrate weddings with great pomp in the eyes of God or men, would certainly matchmake unions between good believers, in their own interest as well as in the interests of their church. The title of Good Men precisely meant also wise men, witnesses, guarantors, counsellors, all for the benefit of these unions of their followers. People before them would exchange free and purely temporal consents. Without any doubt, the wise words of a Good Man would encourage, to certain extent, people to unite by personal inclination or attraction, to the detriment of marriages of convenience. During the brief time when Cathar society could flower more or less normally, meaning especially and almost exclusively in Montségur in the first half of the 13th century, one even saw a definite development of the practice of free unions.

Conversely, the aspirations to a Cathar spirituality could have played a fascinating role for a certain number of women, locked in joyless marriages or weary of the joys of married life.

Medieval women were constantly in labour. It has even been estimated that that this hyper-fertility, which was neither tempered nor restrained by any contraception, was responsible for the very high rate of female mortality in the times. Sanitation was such that each pregnancy was a real risk and each labour a dangerous trial. But in fact it was the unborn child who suffered from this lack of care and hygiene and from the almost yearly labours of women from the age of eighteen. On average only one out of four children survived. Catholic dogma on the subject of reproduction is summed up in the biblical words:

"Grow and multiply . . ."

The aim of Christian marriage was, indeed, to found a family, and the only excuse or motivation for the act of flesh was procreation. Only during recommended Christian periods of abstinence, such as Lent and some religious festivals, could a Catholic mother and spouse hope for a little respite. The Cathar church on the other hand, imposed no rules in this matter. It conceived of things from a totally different logic. Though it did not forbid the act of flesh to its followers and would not have condemned humanity to extinction, as certain malevolent books might have us believe, its doctrine regarding the reproduction of those perishable bodies issued from the void and from evil, owed nothing to this famous "Grow and multiply" of the Old Testament.

Every contraceptive practice was of course forbidden by the church of Rome, since the act of flesh could only escape being labelled a sin when performed by two spouses with the strict goal of procreation. Even more so for practices of abortion, which were akin to evil sorcery. Midwives (the French word translates as 'wise women') have always been under the direst suspicion, from religious authorities, throughout the centuries. Until recent times, the calling of medicine was rarely tolerated in women, owing to the religious fantasy and latent revulsion of males for the 'abortionist' woman, even ore than the 'poison-wielding' woman . . . Let us not awaken old demons - since that is precisely what we are talking about here - and that sleep is still uneasy. Let us only stop to consider that in the Middle Ages, the Cathar church had no reason whatever to condemn to a hell, that it taught did not exist, those of its female believers who sought to terminate one pregnancy too many.

In the conscience of a Catholic pregnant woman, the child she carried appeared as a creature of God, body and soul. However, if the pregnant woman were a Cathar believer, she would probably have been taught that the small weighty body forming in here womb is nothing else, like her own body, than one of those envelopes of flesh that the Devil stitches up, to imprison the angels of God that he stole. She would imagine that at the moment of birth, probably with the first cry, a soul would come to animate the little material body and make it into a complete human being: a divine soul, being one of those souls fallen from the Kingdom of God, and who one day, after many reincarnations, will return there . . . But before birth? The becoming being is no more for her, than flesh coming from the void and doomed to the void. One can surmise how much this nuance would have eased the Christian conscience of the poor women, exhausted by too frequent labours and faced with the temptation of a possible abortion. This does not at all imply that of course the Cathar Good Man, for whom any killing of animals was a sin, would have ever directly encouraged any of his female faithful to voluntarily terminate a pregnancy.

Translated from 'Les Femmes Cathares' by Anne Brenon
Published by Perrin, Paris, 1992
Translation by Marie-Ange Chevrier

d.   Religious rituals

The Cathars believed fervently in a Good God, who was the Lord of all that is celestial, the Heavens, the spirit of Goodness. And they believe that the creation of the material world was the work of a Lesser God, one of God's closest celestial beings, who had broken away and created kingdoms over which he could have dominion. The Lord God Almighty was supreme ruler of the realm of Light, the Lesser God was the Prince of Darkness. Almighty God had dominion over all celestial worlds, the Lesser God created the terrestrial worlds. Spirits of purity, rightfully belonging to the Almighty God, were trapped inside terrestrial bodies, imprisoned there until they could be released.

This Lesser God, this Prince of Darkness, might also be known as the Demiurge or Satan, or the Devil, but these would not necessarily carry the same connotations and overtones that have been imposed by orthodox theologies. Similarly 'evil' to the Cathars was simply all that was not of God. For them, the purpose of life was to achieve perfection and return the spirit imprisoned in material earthly bodies, back to the Realm of Light. Anything else was evil. Spirits that were not released by a life of perfection were condemned to return to Earth, trapped in another form, until such time as release was accomplished.

The Christ of the Cathars is very different from the Christ of the Catholics. For the Cathars, it was misguided to see his mission as an act of Redemption, to redeem the sins of man by his death, but God had sent him to convey a message, to reveal the Truth. The Cathar views of Jesus Christ are a little uncertain, no doubt due to the disinformation put out about their beliefs and the lack of authentic contemporary documentation. Generally, they saw him as being directly from God, the Messenger of God.

God was Good, therefore the Son of God, or the Christ, could not have been human. Cathars were essentially believers in pantheism throughout the celestial realm, that is to say, the Good God had domain over all the heavens, and a sequence of æons was between God himself and the material world, all of which were filled with Divinity.

The Holy Ghost emanated from God as a sort of instrument by means of which divinity could be instilled into creatures. The Son, or the Christ, was chief amongst these æons and as such was sent in a mortal casting to Earth, to combat evil and to rescue the captured spark, release the captive souls in the human bodies. Cathars believed that the Christ æon-being seemed to assume the human form and only seemed to be crucified, for if matter is wholly bad, then a Divine being cannot be made up of such badness. For them the Redemption was an untenable doctrine. Christ taught by example. He showed the way. The Virgin Mary was a figure of little importance. For the Cathars, she was the means by which the Christ-æon passed on its earthly manifestation, the woman whom the Christ-æon used for entrance into the material world.

For them, Christ only had a human resemblance, a 'fantastic body', maybe, and they could point to many passages in the Gospels in support of this phantasmagorical state: walking on the water, appearing to the disciples outside the sepulchre, Christ's miracles. Not being really a man, Christ could not have actually died upon the cross. The Cathars did respect his apparent Passion. They told the story of it in their sermons. But they absolutely avoided worshipping the cross, which they saw as an instrument of torture:

> *"If your father had been hanged, could you then worship the rope and the gibbet on which he had been executed, which had brought about his death?"*

They gave purely spiritual and symbolic meaning to an interpretation of Christ's miracles. When Christ healed the blind, cured the lepers, made the lame to walk, it was understood that by his word he gave them back spiritual insight, he caused them to live again, not physical eyesight, a cure for leprosy or the regaining of mobility. More important, he rendered them receptive to the knowledge, the greater miracle being the truth of their spiritual salvation rather than some temporary repair to their physical body. Similarly, at the Last Supper, the bread and the wine that he distributed to his disciples were only his body and his blood in a purely spiritual sense. They were his message, his Word, his reason for being here. Therefore, the Cathars did not believe in a real presence of the host and they dismissed the Eucharist as being immature idolatry. When they broke bread themselves, in memory of Christ, they did so as an act of homage, not as a communion, in the Catholic sense of the term.

Neither did the Cathars believe in Hell. The 'evil' domain was this world. The Hell was being compelled to remain in this world, kept from returning to the celestial heavens to rejoin the Lord God, where the soul ultimately yearned to be. A soul could only be free if its human wearer lived a life as remote as possible from matter, lived a life of purity. The more pure the life the human lived, the more chance the soul would have of being reunited with God. If a human died without achieving a state of purity, the soul would be reincarnated into another physical prison, another earthly body. Until such time as it was released by a process of purity.

The **Ceremony of Convenenza** was the first initiation rite into Catharism. The celebrant was asked to make one promise, to honour the Perfecti and to be willingly at the disposal of the sect whenever needed. In return there was the promise made to the celebrant of the second initiation rite of Consolamentum, the process by which the celebrant was a candidate to actually become one of the Perfecti. This could even be administered on the deathbed, or sooner, if so desired. It was a severely stringent ritual that required a dedicated and careful preparation. The preparatory process of Abstentia lasted for a year or more and the candidate was carefully examined to be sure of being able to stand the rigours of a Perfecti life.

Consolamentum combined baptism, confirmation and ordination. It took place in a room at some sympathiser's house. A senior Perfectus, or Perfecta, would conduct the ceremony, but others, Perfecti and credentes would be present, including the parents, relatives and friends of the candidate. It was important for the officiating person to be one of the Perfecti, since one needed to have received consolation in order to administer it. The candidate for admission would have been well prepared by the asceticism of the Abstentia, which was more demanding, in its renunciation of all matter, than even the most extreme orthodox orders. The words of the ceremony itself might almost have been written by Catholics. Particular was the importance of the Lord's Prayer, which was almost as used by the orthodox churches. The only thing a Catholic might have thought of as strange was the use of the words 'supersubstantial bread' in place of 'daily bread'

First came the **Servitium**, or **General Confession**, made by the whole congregation, whilst he senior Perfectus held open a copy of the Gospels. The Servitium was apparently recited in the vernacular, but contained nothing heretical, though it did lay stress on the sins of the flesh:

> "Have no mercy on the flesh born in corruption,
> but have mercy on the spirit held in its prison."

There followed the ceremony of the candidate's **Reception of the Lord's Prayer**, with the whole congregation reciting the Lord's Prayer, with the references to 'supersubstantial bread'.

> "If a believer is in abstinence and if the Christians are agreed to administer the Prayer to him, let them wash their hands, and the believers likewise, if there be any."

Everyone washed hands, repeating reverences between actions, whilst the Perfectus next to the senior prepared a table, covering it with a cloth and placing a book upon it.

"Bless us, have mercy upon us", and then said a Melioramentum, bowing down three times towards the ground and saying, in a prostrate manner, before the senior Perfectus: "Bless me."

The Senior replying: "May God bless you" and exhorting the candidate and preaching suitable scriptural verses.

The candidate proclaims: "Lord, pray for me, a sinner, that he may bring me to a good end."

And the senior replies: *"May God bless you and make of you a Good Christian and bring you to a good end."* The senior then hands the candidate the book, admonishing in a long address, again in the vernacular. This admonition consists mostly of quotations from the Gospels and from the Epistle of St Paul, stressing that wherever the church is, there God is, and reminding the candidate that he is before God.

During the ritual, the candidate is referred to as 'Peter' - though the text in the Lyons version of the Consolamentum ritual, it states:

> *"E sil crezent a nom Piere, diza enaissi: En Piere, vos devez entendre..."*
> i.e. *"**If** the believer is called Peter....."*

This may have been a copyist's error or a deliberate attempt to confuse the agents of the Inquisition. It can be taken as reasonably reliable that candidates were referred to as Peter during this ceremony, though just why this should be is not so clear. Possibly to emphasise the Apostolic tradition, to identify all those taking the Consolamentum with the Rock on which Christ's church was to be built.

> A repetition of the Lord's Prayer was followed by a final admonition, urging the candidate to repeat the Prayer constantly throughout life and never to eat or drink without saying it first, and to bear any penance for not doing so.

> The candidate then replied: *"I receive it from God, and from you and from the church."* The candidate and the senior Perfectus then say sixteen Lord's Prayers and performs a 'venia' - a penitential prostration.

There followed the ceremony of the Consolamentum itself. It began with a dialogue between the senior and the candidate, who was asked to renounce the eating of flesh and eggs, lying and swearing, all luxuries and solitude. The candidate took a vow to follow "the rule of Justice and Truth" and takes the book from the hand of the senior.

> *"I give myself to God and to the Church of the Good Christians."*

If the candidate was married, the spouse would then speak, absolving the candidate of all conjugal ties. The promise was then made that not even the threat of death would cause the renunciation of belief or deserting the faith. The promise was made, with a repetition of the Melioramentum. During this last admonition, the candidate was required to renounce the Church of Rome and the Cross made by the Roman priest at baptism, as well as the oil and the chrism used by the Romans.

Once again the senior delivered a long sermon, addressing the candidate as 'Peter'. This was mostly quotations from the New Testament, passages stressing Christ's baptism as a baptism of the spirit.

> *"Peter, you wish to receive the spiritual baptism by which the Holy Spirit is given to the Church of God, together with the Holy Prayer and the imposition of hands by Good Men. Of this baptism our Lord Jesus Christ says in the Gospel of St Matthew to his disciples: 'Go therefore, teach all the nations, baptising them in the name of the Father, and of the Son, and of the Holy Spirit, teaching them to observe all things whatsoever I have commanded you; and behold I am with you all days, even to the consummation of the world.' And in the Gospel of St Mark, He says: 'Go ye into the whole world and preach the gospel to every creature. He that believeth and is baptised shall be saved; but he that believeth not shall be condemned.' And in the Gospel of St John, He says to Nicodemus: 'Amen, amen, I say to thee, unless a men be born again of the water and the Holy Spirit, he cannot enter into the Kingdom of God.' And John the Baptist spoke of this baptism, when he said, 'I baptise you with water with water but he that shall come after me is mightier than I, the latchet of whose shoes I am not worthy to loose. He shall baptise you in the Holy Spirit and fire.' And Jesus says, in the Acts of the Apostles, 'For John indeed baptised with water, but you shall be baptised with the Holy Spirit.'"*

The candidate was admonished to keep all of Christ's commandments, to hate the world and its works:

> *"No one shall enter the Kingdom of God unless reborn of the water and of the Holy Spirit"* - 'water' being used as a symbol of the 'Spirit'.

> *"Behold, I have given you power to tread upon serpents and scorpions and upon all the power of the enemy; and nothing shall hurt you."*

The candidate accepted the homily, once more performed the Melioramentum, this time with the Perfectus who was the sponsor of the candidate. The candidate was then given the 'tradition', that is, the 'Book and Dominical Prayers, the New Testament and the Word of the Lord. Confession having been made, the candidate knelt before the senior, who placed a Gospel on the candidate's head, saying first three parcias, then two adoremus, and finally a benediction in Latin:

> *"Holy Father, take Thy servant in Thy justice and send Thy grace and Holy Spirit upon Thy catechumen."*

The senior then pronounced six *Paternosters* and three *adoremus*, the Lord's Prayer and the first seventeen verses of St John's Gospel, read in Latin.

The congregation then repeated *adoremus, gratia* and three *parcias*. Then everyone performed the Kiss of Peace, then kissed the Gospel, repeated the Lord's Prayer sixteen times and closed with a *veniæ*.

The ceremony was the same, whatever the sex of the candidate, save for one or two minor verbal changes and care for Perfectus and candidate of opposite sex never to actually come into physical contact. Consolamentum delivered on the deathbed was considerably curtailed, according to circumstance and the discretion of the senior Perfectus administering the ceremony. A sick person would receive the sacrament without leaving the sickbed.

During periods of persecution, the Ceremony Consolamentum had to be administered in a clandestine way, with only two Perfecti present, brought secretly and generally by night, by loyal agents of the Cathar church.

The Book of the Two Principles

One of the most complete texts to have survived the Catholic determination to destroy everything Cathar is a treatise written sometime in the mid-thirteenth century by an Italian Cathar. The surviving manuscript, discovered in a Dominican convent in San Marco and now lodged in the Biblioteca Nazionale of the city of Florence, appears to be the work of two scribes. It is believed by some scholars to have been a summary of a longer work, written about 1230. The most likely author of this longer work, or at least a major part of it, was John of Lugio, a doctor and leader of one of the 'true Christians' sects, the Albanenses, prevalent in the vicinity of Lake Guarda, between Brescia and Verona.

'The Book of Two Principles' was discovered, as an authentic piece of Cathar writing, and edited by Antoine Dondaine, around 1939. René Nelli translated the work into French.

The treatise consists of seven parts and constitutes the most considerable body of Catharist literature to come to light. The intention of the author appears to have been to affirm certain principles as they related to his own Albanenses sect. Six of the parts are concerned with the problem posed by the existence of evil amongst those creatures of God, the angels, when God was pure goodness. How could angels who were created good have been turned to evil? The final seventh part is a compilation of scriptural verses, showing that the true followers of Christ must inevitably be persecuted. The author attempts to account for the existence of evil amongst good by asserting an absolute duality of gods, creators and creation and by denying free will in the creatures of good.

The work is somewhat disjointed, repetitive and contradictory, lacking the clarity and precision of some of the better orthodox texts of the period. But what it lacks in clarity, it more than makes up for in passion and conviction. It is important in that it is one of the few authentic Cathar texts to have survived and is thus able to give us some insight into the theological arguments that distinguish Catharism from other forms of Christianity. There were no doubt numerous other Catharist texts written and probably many of them would have been on a par with orthodox theologies in the clarity and precision of their arguments, but persecution and inquisition zealously destroyed them.

The author of the 'Book of Two Principles' must have been familiar with the Bible in its vulgate text and a few phrases reminiscent of the Catharist ritual in Latin indicate his familiarity with that work. Presumably he had also read works by another Cathar sect, the Garantenses, for he directs part V of the treatise in argument against them. He also makes reference to an orthodox opponent, whom he appears to hold in great respect, calling him Master William. This was most probably William of Auvergne, Bishop of Paris, who died in 1249. Other 'opponents of the truth' he refers to as 'the unlearned' or 'the unenlightened', calling theirs 'the belief if the ignorant'. He wrote for the benefit of those attempting to be 'true Christians' who are 'hampered in rightly understanding the truth' and he wrote for 'the instruction of beginners', taking their first steps towards its true comprehension.

A Summary of the 'Book of Two Principles':

I. **On Free Will** - The author states the necessity of Two Principles and argues for a cause of evil other than God. Those opposed to the true concept of the Two Principles state that there is only one God, who is pure, good, omniscient, and omnipotent. But there is a difficulty arising from this tenet, because we know that God's angelic creatures fell into sin. Since God's knowledge embraces all that was, is, and shall be, He would have known that His angels would sin, before the event. But if God had rendered his angels to be only perfect, they would have been unable to sin or to do evil, but the Lord would have 'given them no thanks for their service because they would have been unable to do otherwise'. Because of this knowledge, their sin was inevitable, for knowledge and will are synonymous in God. Consequently, it must be concluded that there is a cause of evil other than the goodness of God.

The various arguments of the 'opponents of the truth' are intended to prove that the angels sinned out of choice and not out of necessity, but these arguments are refuted. That we may carry out God's will by serving Him in His creation proves that He is beset by the enemy, although that service does not arise from our will, but from His. The absolute opposition of good in relation to evil must be emphasised. It is axiomatic that no power can exist equally capable of good and evil at the same time; if it did, the angels having it could not avoid doing evil, for which God would have the ultimate responsibility - a wicked thought! If an evil cause did not exist, no evil result would be produced. If the angels had free will by God's creation, and He knew that they would sin, their sin was inevitable and consequently attributable to God himself. William of Auvergne argues that, since God could not make His angels as perfect as Himself, they must covet His perfection - but this argument is rejected.

II.   On Creation - To support the conclusion that there must be two creator-gods, the scriptural evidence of is used. 'Opponents of the truth' insist on the omnipotence and eternity of God, the sole creator. These people are not able to understand the true meanings of the words 'create' and 'make'. 'Creation' does not mean to bring something out of nothing, for all matter exists, for all time, with its creator. Properly understood, 'creation' embraces three modes of change:

> (a) that which is already good is changed for the better; thus, Christ and the other angels were 'created' by God as ministers to those who had sinned;

> (b) 'to create' means that those who have fallen under the domination of evil may be changed, 'created' again to good, and redeemed by the illumination afforded them by Christ;

> (c) it may mean that the good God allows His enemy to afflict His people, for a time, to achieve His own purposes. Each of these ideas is well attested by scriptural authority, but in no sense is God thought to be the source of any evil that exists.

III.   On the Terms of Universality - The threefold aspect of creation is confirmed by an examination of the concept of universals. Terms satisfying universality in the Bible must be properly interpreted. One who has wisdom will perceive that such words as 'all' and 'every' are not all-embracing. Sometimes they refer to all that is good, sometimes to all that is evil, sometimes to all that was once good but fell under the influence of evil and will be redeemed. The conclusion is reiterated: 'All' that is evil cannot be the same as 'all' that is good, nor can it arise from the same source; therefore two separate sources and influences must be postulated.

IV.   A Compend for the Instruction of Beginners - Concerning creation, the terms 'Heaven' and 'Earth' used in the Scriptures refer to the intelligent creatures of the good God, the spiritual creation. The good God is not the creator of the base and tangible elements of this world; another creator is responsible for them. God is Almighty, but not in the sense that He can create evil; what He does not desire He cannot do. He is omnipotent over all good things, but there is another creator from whom all evil flows, who in no way derives from the good God. The evil one is eternal, as are his works. The scriptures prove this. To him belongs all the wickedness reported in the Old Testament: adultery, murder, theft, falsehoods, broken promises, and in the New Testament, the persecution of Christ.

V.   Against the Garantenses - The Garantenses were another Catharist sect, more commonly known by contemporaries as the sect of Concorezzo, who seemed not to fully embrace the dualist concept. The author makes a strong rebuttal of their theology. The Garantenses believe that there is one God, creator of all, but that an evil lord, God's creature, made this world. There is no support this by Divine testimony, for believing that the evil lord was creator of the Old Testament, how can they then use this as evidence? Or, even if they use its arguments, how can they avoid the plain testimony to be found in the Old Testament that the evil one was a creator? The Garantenses are challenged to debate the issue. And another question is posed: How can they uphold the belief in creation as the work of a good God and still defy His responsibility for the evil they discern in this world?

VI.   On Will - Returning to the themes discussed in the first part, this section reiterates the discourse 'On Free Will'. How can free will be justified in the case of those who never have done, do not and never will do good? If God did not know that angels would become demons, He was not omniscient; if He did know their fate, they could not avoid it, for his knowledge extends all that of necessity occurs. Furthermore, those who believe in free will and believe that new souls are daily being created fall into grave error. How many there would be who would be unable, because they were infants or were hampered by bodily infirmities, to do good and to merit salvation! Hence the concept of free will is untenable.

VII.   On Persecution - Christ is the shepherd who sought to recover the lost sheep. He suffered for their sake, but His suffering did not come from the good God. Instead this wickedness was endured by the good God in order to accomplish His purpose, the redemption of His people. As Christ and the prophets suffered from the evil one's domination, so must all true Christians suffer, returning good for evil, for all who will live in Christ must first endure persecution.

See also 'The Theology of the Two Principles' by Michel Roquebert in Chapter 19.

Chapter 13
HERETICS AT LARGE

The Catholic church had made spasmodic efforts to quell the rise of Catharism and to intimidate its followers, to convert credentes back to the Catholic faith. A number of Papal legates were sent to the region to unearth 'heretics' and bring them to book. For all sorts of reasons it is difficult for us to know precisely what Cathar faith actually was. Not only was it to suffer a peculiarly violent demise, but it was also subjected to a systematic process of denigration, slander and distortion. The Catholic church preached against Catharism with vehement polemic, destroyed its written records, surrounded it with a plethora of disinformation and downright lies. However, some aspects of the faith have come down to us in a way in which we can begin to untangle some of the truth from the subterfuge.

Cathars were great preachers and made no secret of their beliefs. They took part regularly in theological debates and argued with bishops and visiting legates. Many such public discourses are recorded from 1176, with Bernard of Clairvaux, later to become St Bernard, one of the earliest preachers sent to turn the population way from Cathar faith, and later, the great missionary campaigns of 1204-6, conducted by Dominic Guzman, later to become St Dominic, and his companions. From such records we can deduce that the Cathars were mighty orators, passionate logicians, knowledgeable theologians and sincere seekers after the truth. They did not hide behind vague and ineffable mysteries that could not be revealed to the profane, but claimed their doctrine rested on sound, reasonable common sense and a devout belief in the absolute spirituality of God. They attacked the mysteries of the Catholic church, which they charged with being mere superstition and magic. The Cathars declared themselves the heirs of a tradition that was older than that held by the church of Rome., being less contaminated and nearer in spirit to the

Apostolic tradition. They could claim to be the only persons to have kept and cherished the Holy Spirit which Christ had bestowed upon his church.

The Cathar doctrine was not merely proselytising, but was truly evangelical, endeavouring to put into place a literal and practical application of its principles and doctrines. The ministers of the Cathar church, the 'bishops and priests' of the Cathar faith, the Perfecti, were very powerful and effective preachers. They wooed the population, easily converting them, due to the profound disillusionment with the Catholic clergy. The financial and administrative side of the church's organisation was in the hands of the ordinary credentes, who had not renounced the material world. These ranged from rich merchants and doctors of medicine, to peasants, artisans, farm labourers and shopkeepers.

Legend has it that at one of these great public debates between Dominic Guzman, who was destined to become St Dominic, and the senior Cathar Perfecti, which took place at Montréal, near Fanjeaux, a miracle took place. After several hours of debate in which both sides held their own, theologically, morally and spiritually, Dominic asked that the Cathars and the Catholics each subject one of their texts to ordeal by fire. The Cathar parchment, said to be a rendition of God's judgement, perished in the flames. The Catholic parchment, on the other hand, three times floated above the flames and then shot to the roof, burning one of the beams very badly. Reputedly, this same burned beam can still be seen in the church at Fanjeaux.

A more rational and sober account of the same event has been recorded by William de Puylaurens. Dominic and his long-standing preaching companion, the Bishop of Osma, were up against one of the greatest of all the Cathar orators and preachers, Guilhabert de Castres, who was filius maior to the Catharist Bishop of Toulouse, at that time, and other Cathars, including one Arnald Hot. William de Puylaurens makes no mention of parchments on fire, but makes a thorough report of the debate:

> *"The Cathar Arnald Hot maintained that: '....the Church of Rome, as defended by the Bishop of Osma, was neither holy nor the Bride of Christ; rather it espoused of the Devil and its doctrine diabolical. It was that Babylon that St John called, in his Apocalypse, the mother of fornications and abominations, drunk with the blood of the Saints and of Christ's martyrs. Moreover, the Bishop's ordination was neither sanctified nor valid nor, indeed, established by Our Lord Jesus Christ. Christ and his Apostles had never ordained or laid down the Canon of Mass as it now existed.'*

> *The Bishop of Osma offered contrary proof, citing evidence from the New Testament: 'O dolorous case! To think that amongst Christians the ordinances of the Church and of the Catholic faith should have fallen into such disregard that secular judges were called upon to pronounce on such blasphemies!'"*

The judges who had been called on to give a verdict in this debate found themselves so divided that they were discharged without having come to any decision whatsoever. It was left to the public relations machine of the Catholic church to come up with floating parchments and burned beams, in order to salvage anything from this encounter.

St Dominic is always presented to us as a the sincere and humble man, one of the first to adopt the humility of poverty and a devout monastic life. For sure, he did live a life as austere and devoted as those of the Perfecti of the Cathar church. From a religious family, he was ordained into the priesthood and became an Austin canon of Osma cathedral. His first seven years as a priest were largely uneventful, devoting himself to prayer and penance. In 1204 he first met a Cathar 'heretic', at Toulouse. He was impressed by the simplicity of their lives, the passion of their conviction. As a devout Catholic, he also was convinced of misguided nature of their beliefs. The wrong believer is perhaps worse than the unbeliever. At least the latter is something of a lost cause, but the 'heretic' has shown tendencies of being drawn towards the faith, but has then tried to subvert it, to distort its true meaning. Surely such people should be brought back to the fold, by prayer, by discourse, by persuasion, and by force, if necessary.

Dominic founded the nunnery at Prouille, realising that if women were a force to be reckoned with in the Cathar communities, women may be the most effective persuaders in the Catholic cause. However, the declaration of Crusade by Pope Innocent III in 1208 changed the course of events over the next years. Dominic expressed distaste for the violence and massacres perpetrated against the Cathar region and he continued to use instruction and prayer. He refused three offers to become a Bishop during this period.

The last seven years of his life were occupied with the founding of the order that was to carry his name. This was at the birth of the monastic surge that was to be a feature of the later part of the Middle Ages. Francis of Assisi was founding in similar order of poor friars in Italy. The emphasis of the orders founded by these sincere and devout men was on communities which would be centres of sacred learning, whose adherents would spend their lives in study, teaching, preaching a prayer. They gave the Catholic church a devout face to show the world, a model to rival the austere tradition established by the Cathars and the Bogomils. It is perhaps ironic that both orders became embroiled in the setting up of the Inquisition. Their participation was no doubt motivated by the highest ideals, but the forty-five stringent canons that had been formulated in order to purge the region of 'heretics' were to become almost as severe as the sieges and massacres of the Crusade. For the next century almost, people in the small hamlets and villages in the mountainous regions of the Languedoc lived in fear of being accused by the Inquisition of 'heresy', of associating with, knowing any, consorting with, shielding and assisting, or giving succour to, any 'persons thought to be heretic'. The Inquisition was probably the longest witch-hunt of all time.

More of that later, after the Crusade. Back in 1204, Dominic Guzman had set his sights on converting the Cathars back to the orthodox cause. Over the next two years seven large scale public debates were held, in which Dominic and a group of Cistercian legates confronted the champions of Catharism. The last of these debates was held at Pamiers in the castle of the Count of Foix, whose sister Esclarmonde, herself an initiated Cathar, took part. She had received the Consolamentum and had founded a convent for Catharist women. Dominic was more effective than some of the religious leaders who had preached to the Cathar credentes. He had energy and zeal and people were impressed by the sincerity of his life. He effected a few converts, but by and large the Cathar faith remained firm and the higher reaches of the Papal establishment were becoming a trifle impatient.

The Pope instructed Count Raymond VI of Toulouse and Viscount Raymond-Roger of Béziers and Carcassonne to root out the heretics in their lands. To his extreme distaste, both of them refused to do so. Neither was a Cathar himself, but they respected the rights of the majority of their Countrymen to worship as they wished. It seemed to them that the Papacy and the King of France, with his friends, the Northern barons, were ganging up on the Cathars and possibly even against the Languedoc. Suspicion was rife and feelings were running high. Many Southerners, Catholics as well as Cathars, rallied behind their leaders. In January 1208, Count Raymond invited the Papal legate, Pierre de Castlenau, to Toulouse for discussions. Talks did not go well. At first, Raymond showed signs of accommodating the wishes of the church, but when pressed into making a commitment to use force against his own people, he lost his temper and threatened Pierre de Castlenau with his life, if he did not leave his lands immediately.

However, before they could leave the Languedoc, the Papal Legate and his entourage were attacked and Pierre de Castlenau was stabbed in the back. The Pope, Innocent III, immediately pronounced this an act of 'terrorism', carried out by human monsters. This somewhat ignores the fact that the Pope had dispatched his legate to persuade the Southern lords to murder thousands of their own people. Like modern interpretations of 'terrorism', it depends where you are standing as to who the 'terrorists' actually are.

The following day, Pope Innocent III wrote a letter to the faithful Catholics of the South, telling them the story of Pierre de Castlenau's tragic death, presenting him as a martyr and fully implicating Count Raymond VI of Toulouse in his murder. There was no proof of this, but in the current struggle, the stakes were high.

Chapter 14
PERSECUTING THE CATHARS: STORIES, MYTHS AND LEGENDS

a.   The Albigensian Crusade

On 28th March 1208, Pope Innocent III flung down a Bull of Anathema on the rich soil of the Languedoc, a solemn and necessary call to arms against a population that had strayed from the true path, summoning all Christian nations to launch a Crusade against these 'heretics':

> "*Since the church in that region sits in a sadness and grief with no one to comfort her, after the death of that just man, and it is said that the faith there has disappeared, that peace has perished, that the plague of heresy and the fury of the enemy have grown stronger and stronger and that, unless she is strongly supported against such an attack, the ship of the Church will seem to have been wrecked in that place almost completely, we advise all of you most urgently, encourage you fervently and in so great a crisis of need, enjoin you confidently in the strength of Christ, granting remission of sins, not to delay in making haste to combat so may evils and to make it your business to bring to peace those people, in the name of him who is the God of Peace and Love.*"

In the Catholic mind of the Holy See, this Crusade was justifiable and necessary because the people who lived in the Languedoc posed a greater threat to the Christian church than the infidels who had dared to inhabit the sacred and revered places of the Holy Land that previous crusades had reigned against. These people were 'worse than the very Saracens'. The army of the Crusade assembled at Burgundy in the spring of 1209.

The Crusaders travelled, military commanders and religious leaders on horseback, soldiers on foot, down the Rhône valley. 100,000 men, under the orders of the Papal legate, Arnaud-Amery, Abbé de Cîteaux. This vast force included some of the most renowned nobles in the kingdom, the Duke of Burgundy, the counts of Saint-Pol and Nevers, the Seneschal of Anjou and Countless prelates. Also in the ranks was one Simon de Montfort, who had travelled from his home in the Chevreuse Valley. Simon was a man of principle. He had fought in earlier crusades, but had refused to follow the Fourth Crusade, which had been ordered to launch an attack on the ancient Byzantine city of Constantinople, under the instructions of the Doge of Venice. He had principles and had firmly refused to attack the Christians of Constantinople. But now, the Pope's appeal to drive out the 'devil within' touched his sensibilities and Simon de Montfort joined the Crusade against the Cathars, sincerely believing he was engaged in God's work. It is in such misguided sincerity that Holy War is rooted. We will hear a lot more of Simon de Montfort.

The actual army of the Crusade was made up of anybody and everybody - drunks, thieves, ne'er-do-wells, criminals. Participation in the Crusade gave absolution to all sins, past, present and future - it was literally license to kill. Not only that, but lands designated for invasion were declared 'free for anybody who could capture them'. This normally meant the nobles in charge of invading forces, but there was always the odd chance of capturing loot and bounty.

Along with the thousands of knights were many thousands of footsoldiers, from all parts of France and elsewhere. Amongst these were the routiers, notoriously brutal mercenary soldiers, most of them Basques or Aragonese, known for their immoral, cruel and outrageous behaviour, even by horrific crusading standards. These routiers were officially forbidden by the Catholic church, but this never prevented leaders of crusades from employing them in vast numbers. Also in the ranks of the crusading army were brigands from the 'Cour de Miracles', the haunt of criminals in Paris. Fired by impassioned sermons by the Pope's envoys, all crusaders were convinced that theirs was a noble cause. They were to root out 'heresy' from the lands and defend the 'true faith'. At the head of this collection of jealous noblemen and unruly brigands was a clerk, a man whose stubborn nature verged on madness, with a disturbing cruel streak, a man from the Languedoc who was well aware of what was at stake, politically and on the part of the church. His name was Arnaud-Amaury. He was the Abbé de Cîteaux and a Papal legate.

Languedoc went about its daily business, generally unaware of what was brewing outside its borders. However, Raymond VI was fully aware of the situation. In June 1209, at Saint-Gilles-du-Gard, homeland of the counts of Toulouse and where Pierre de Castlenau had been killed, Raymond agreed to accept the authority of the church and to submit to flagellation and humiliation before the representatives of the Pope. It was a way of demonstrating to the people how great and good was the church, representing the might and majesty of God.

In the great church of Saint-Gilles, there were gathered three archbishops, nineteen bishops, a great throng of other church dignitaries and nobles, thousands of ordinary people, crowding the church and the square outside. This was a church spectacle, designed to demonstrate just who was in charge. Raymond, Count of Toulouse, with a chord round his neck, a candle in his hand and wearing the penitent's garb, was brought into the square and stripped to the waist. After swearing allegiance to the Pope and to all the legates, he was given Absolution and then flogged, with birch twigs.

Raymond VI even went so far as to join the Crusade. He was neither mad, a coward, nor a traitor. He was just making the best of a bad job, coming to terms with the situation as it existed. As a volunteer to the Crusade, his lands would be safe from confiscation.

Within days, the Crusade was on the move, marching to the South.

By 21st July 1209, this vast armed force stood outside the city gates of Béziers, just inland from the Golfe du Lion in the Mediterranean. Béziers stands proudly on a rocky promontory, the river Orb below and in the distance, the plains of Hérault and the vineyards that for centuries have been so important to the local region. This handsome walled town was strategically important, as a trading base and a gateway into the mainland. The Papal legate refused Trencavel, Viscount of Béziers, the right to be reconciled with the Roman Catholic church. The crusaders demanded of the town that 222 named 'heretics' should be handed over to them. They refused to open gates. The refusal proved extremely costly.

The gates were taken by assault, were breached, and the unruly throng burst into the town. The massacre that followed was sickening in its extent and depravity. No one was spared. When asked, "How will we recognise the Cathars?" Arnaud-Amaury is reputed to have said:

> *"Kill them all, the Lord will recognise his own!"*

Kill them all, the Lord will recognise his own! The Crusade against the Cathars had begun. Whether the words attributed to the Papal legate are true or not, they do reflect the atrocity that was perpetrated in Béziers that Summer afternoon of 1209, which was very real and which he confirmed in a letter to the Pope:

"Our forces put to the sword almost twenty thousand people."

He could have added that some four thousand of these were massacred whilst taking refuge in the Church of St Mary Magdalene, the priest there being the first to be put to the sword as he stood in the doorway, cross in hand, vainly attempting to appeal for his flock. He could have also added that amongst the slaughtered were women, children, old people, the ill and infirm. No one was spared.

The butchery carried out that day at Béziers sent a cold chill throughout the region. It also resulted in a strong sense of unity. The Catholics of Languedoc did not flock to the ranks of the Crusade in great numbers. Instead, many of them joined forces, defending the 'heretics'.

The Chanson de la Croisade Albigeoise, one of the only contemporary accounts of the Crusade, records a lull after this gruesome storm:

> *"For three days the Crusaders rested in grassy meadows, on the banks of the River Orb, and on the fourth day they departed again, knights and sergeants all together, across the open Country. Ensigns were raised and streaming in the wind and nothing would stop their advances."*

The people of Narbonne, having heard of the savage butchery in neighbouring Béziers, surrendered in terror, even before the Crusade had arrived on their doorstep. The Crusade was met by a deputation from Narbonne, led by archbishop Bérenger and the Viscount

Aimery. They promised full and complete submission and a complete willingness to co-operate in the repression of the 'heretics'.

Six days march and the massed forces of the Crusade were outside the walls of Carcassonne. Raymond-Roger Trencavel, Viscount of this district, as well as the fallen Béziers, entrenched himself with an army of loyal knights and the population of the city. Carcassonne was regarded as impregnable. Fifteen days of siege followed. Frightful heat and drought. Water rationed. Animals dying. Rotting carcasses. Swarms of meat flies. Stench.

Under a promise of a negotiated settlement, Raymond-Roger Trencavel presented himself at the Crusader's encampment to negotiate terms, but was immediately taken prisoner, being fist imprisoned in the dungeons of his own castle, whilst his city was forcibly taken, and then murdered in his prison cell.

The Papal orders were obeyed to the letter. The prelates of the Crusade, with the Abbé Arnaud-Amaury in authority, declared that Trencavel was stripped of his titles and dispossessed

The Medieval walled-city of Carcassonne

Béziers from the River Orb

of his estates. These were then offered to anyone who wanted them. All of the titles, lands and estates fell to a lord from l'Ille de France, noted for his courage in warfare, Simon de Montfort, who was, amongst his many nominal titles, Earl of Leicester, although he had never set foot on English soil. De Montfort had fought in the Fourth Crusade, but had left that military campaign when it was decided to attack the Christian stronghold of Constantinople. He was a deeply religious man and had taken up the cause of the Holy War in order to defend Christendom against Saracen 'filth'. But he drew the line at fighting Christians and returned home before the attack on Constantinople.

However, he seemed to have no such qualms now, and he became head of the all these vast military invasion forces. As the new Viscount of Carcassonne, he made that city his military headquarters for the remainder of the campaign.

Following the lead of Dominic Guzman, at least in matching his conviction that he was bringing straying 'heretics' back into the fold, de Montfort hoped to strike at the heart of Catharism by marching on Fanjeaux. He spent the autumn launching raids to the North, towards Castres and Albi, where the Catholic Bishop opened his doors to him. To the South, he advanced on Limoux, Mirepoix and Pamiers, where he was received with full honours by the abbé.

De Montfort was welcomed as a liberator by a clergy that expected him to restore the authority of the Catholic church and force the population of the region back to the straight road of orthodoxy. However, in the eyes of the consulates and landed gentry, he was simply a foreign conqueror, come to snatch their possessions. In the eyes of the common people, he was a deadly scourge, leading an unruly army that destroyed all it encountered, pillaged, stole, raped, robbed, burnt crops, massacred flocks, hanged and tortured peasants, despising the sanctity of life. The horrors of war fell on the Catholic as well as the Cathar, on the humble as well as the powerful, there was no flicker of discrimination in a Crusade.

The villages and towns that fell into the hands of the Crusaders were distributed by Simon de Montfort to his high-ranking companion knights. Lambert de Thury got Limoux, Bouchard de Marly was given Saissac and Gui de Levis became lord of Mirepoix. All this was in line with Papal directives. A few local lords, either through fear of losing their possessions or by a sincere loyalty to the Catholic faith, swore allegiance to de Montfort and to the Crusade, sometimes joining the ranks themselves, hoping for benefits in return. Others, the majority in fact, took to their heels, abandoning their property and possessions. Many withdrew to Toulouse with their families.

Simon de Montfort

These dispossessed nobles, who had lost their estates in the hurricane intensity of the 1209 campaign, regrouped at Cabaret, where we now find the chateaux of Lastours, at Minerve, and at Termes. From these bases, for months on end, they boldly attacked the rear of de Montfort's army, intercepting his convoys, ambushing his troops and even launching commando raids on his depot of arsenals and siege stores that had been built on the banks of the Aude, under the ramparts of Carcassonne. This guerrilla activity briefly prevented de Montfort from pushing forwards. It was made worse by his knowing that these pockets of resistance were also shielding Cathar Perfecti, who had escaped ahead of the advancing Crusade. The leader of the Crusade launched an attack on Cabaret, but it was a pathetic failure.... At the height of the summer, de Montfort laid siege to Minerve, which surrendered after several weeks, largely because their water had run out. Revenge for the resistance was swift. One hundred and forty Cathar Perfecti, both Parfaits and Parfaites, were publicly burned.

The invading Crusaders then moved on, to wreak havoc on Termes, in the mountain region of the Corbières. There again, lack of water led to a surrender, but only after a fierce resistance lasting nearly four months. The fall of the town was marked by yet another savage massacre. The noble lord of Termes was thrown into prison in Carcassonne, where he died three years later. The Crusade took Coustaussa and Albedun on the way to Puivert, which in turn surrendered after a mere three days.

A few weeks later, Cabaret, now completely isolated, negotiated an honourable surrender, thus completing the conquest of all of Trencavel's domains. Simon de Montfort now set his sights on the County of Toulouse.

At the end of March 1211, he besieged Lavaur, to which the Perfecti and several knights of the Cabaret resistance has withdrawn. After five weeks of particularly vicious fighting, the town was taken by storm. Four hundred Parfaits and Parfaites were executed - the largest public burning of the entire period of the Crusade. The lady of the town, the Dame Guiraude, was raped, thrown down a well and then stoned, battered and buried alive, under large boulders. As an additional piece of discreditable revenge, and in defiance of all rules of warfare, all the captured knights had their throats cut.

The capture of Lavaur started the conquest of all the Lauragais and the Albigeois. Six weeks of crashing attack on intervening towns and villages brought the Crusaders in front of the ramparts of Toulouse. The whole circumference of the city was put under siege, but after fifteen days the defenders forced de Montfort to withdraw. This rallied neighbouring princes, feudal lords, friends and relations of the Count of Toulouse, who allied to put up stern resistance. Also Lauragais and Albigeois staged resurgence against the Crusade. Such alliances were effective and it took de Montfort six months to make up lost ground. He made his main objective the isolation of Toulouse, meanwhile making significant conquests in the surrounding territory. Realising the danger, Raymond VI, the Count of Toulouse, sought the aid of his brother-in-law, Pierre II, Count of Barcelona and King of Aragon. The Catholic king came on board with all his knights and extensive military resources, but even these combined forces were not enough to defeat de Montfort and the Crusaders, and the coalition was defeated on the plains of Muret in September 1213.

Raymond VI was condemned and banished to exile. Simon de Montfort was installed as the new Count of Toulouse. But Raymond merely moved to Provence and within two years had raised another army against the Crusade. De Montfort left to oppose the revolt and whilst he was away, the people of Toulouse took advantage of his absence and rose in rebellion. Back came de Montfort, subduing the revolt and severely punishing the townspeople. However, the other revolt, in Provence, was gaining steam and de Montfort was forced to redirect his forces to that region. Seizing the opportunity, Raymond VI, together with his son, the future Raymond VII, triumphantly entered Toulouse. When de Montfort returned, he found the town armed to the teeth. He laid siege, but the resistance was fired with a new found fervour. The siege lasted for ten months, ending only when Simon de Montfort himself was killed, his head being shattered by a rock from a catapult, operated, as legend has it, by the women of Toulouse.

Simon de Montfort's son, Amaury, young and courageous, but without the experience of his father, took over as head of the Crusade, as well as acquiring all his father's titles. He did not have much idea of how to deal with the determined forces of liberation launched by the southern princes and their vassals. In January 1224, after losing vast territories taken by his father, he found himself under siege in Carcassonne. The forces ranged against him included the Count of Toulouse, the Count of Foix and Raymond Trencavel, younger son of Trencavel, the former Viscount of Carcassonne, who had been defeated in 1209 and subsequently murdered. The latest Trencavel was now about to avenge his father. He had come back from exile in Catalonia to be in at the kill. There was no kill, however, as Amaury de Montfort meekly surrendered and returned to the North of France, with the last of his loyal followers.

Those Perfecti who had escaped death at the stake during the Crusade, gradually returned home as the crusaders abandoned the region. The hierarchy of the Cathar church, ravaged by fifteen years of war and decimated by the burnings, started to reopen the 'houses', their places of worship and work, and to resume their public preaching. Catharism benefited from the hatred felt for the Catholic invaders and gained an even stronger position in the region than they had held before the Crusade. A fifth Bishopric had to be opened in Razès, to accommodate the upsurge of new followers. Fifteen years of barbarous executions and torture had achieved nothing, except to strengthen the position of the Cathar church.

The restoration of peace did not last long. After much discussion, and no doubt smarting with the embarrassing humiliation of defeat, King Louis VIII and the new Pope, Honorius III, finally agreed on the necessity of yet another Crusade. This time it would be the king himself who led the campaign. It set out in the spring of 1226.

The battered and exhausted towns and villages of the Languedoc had no stomach for another protracted struggle against such vicious forces. Lords of small towns surrendered to the Catholic prelates, even before the forces of the king had arrived in the region. The only areas willing and able to gird their loins for further resistance were Toulouse, under Raymond VII, some towns to the north of Carcassonne, Cabaret, and, in the South, Limoux and the Razès Country, where guerrillas installed themselves ready for the fight.

But the military battalions gathered against them were far too formidable. The imbalance of forces resulted in early submission, which was ratified in Paris on Maundy Thursday 1229, when Raymond VII signed the articles of surrender. Most of the regions of the Languedoc became provinces of the crown. Raymond was allowed to keep the Toulouse, Agenais and Quercy regions, but the treaty provided for their future annexation by the royal domain by forcing Jeanne de Toulouse, daughter and sole heir of the Count, to marry the brother of the king, Saint Louis.

At the end of 1229 a council was assembled in Toulouse to put into operation the necessary security and judicial arrangements for the suppression of Catharism. The religion of the Bons-Hommes and Bonnes-Dames was forced underground, driven into a clandestine phase from which it would never again emerge.

The Northern knights had sacked the Country of the South, but had settled nothing on the religious plane. Where they had failed, the Inquisition was to succeed. In the ensuing years, Raymond VII tried to cheat the Holy See and the Crown of France by crafty diplomacy, to

attempt to restore his power, to thwart the harsh conditions and clauses of the Treaty of Paris and to frustrate the excessive powers of the Inquisition.

In the summer of 1240, Raymond Trencavel returned from his second exile in Catalonia, crossing the Pyrénées and rallying to his side the Corbières nobility, including Guillaume de Peyrepertuse, Pierre de Cucugnan, Pierre de Fenouillet, and Olivier de Termes. He descended through the valley of the Aude, rejoicing has his army rapidly swelled with inhabitants of the towns and villages, who joined his colours, as the entourage passed through Limoux, Montréal, Montolieu. It was a mass rising. When they saw the power of this rapidly growing force, other nobles, including Pierre-Roger of Cabaret, Arnaud of Aragon, Guillaume of Capendu, and a host of others, rallied to his ranks. The objective was clear: to dislodge from Carcassonne the imposed vassal of the King and regain control of the city. The siege of the city, the third in thirty-one years, lasted for thirty-four days. But this time it ended in failure. The King of France, Saint Louis, despatched a powerful army, commanded by his chamberlain, Jean de Beaumont. Fearful of being taken from the rear, Trencavel withdrew, but got his forces cornered in Montréal, where he was besieged by de Beaumont. The counts of Toulouse and Foix came to offer their services as mediators. Trencavel and his followers were able to negotiate and to leave in safety, ostensibly taking the road to another Catalonian exile. However, this time they were cheated. Royal troops ambushed them, right in the heart of the Corbières, and without mercy, they routed Trencavel's entourage, sacking the places that gave them refuge and routinely hanging all prisoners.

By mid-November, the retreating army had settled at the château built on the formidable rock of Peyrepertuse, but were in no fit state to endure another siege. When the royal forces arrived, Guillaume de Peyrepertuse delivered up his fortress and surrendered officially. Trencavel himself once more left for exile in Catalonia and several of his companions returned home to negotiate their pardons with the king.

This uprising had given the King of France food for thought. The Languedoc had been annexed for barely ten years, yet in that time it had shown itself to be very poorly protected. Now he would need to take steps against all potential revolt and the possible aggressive return of hostile exiles. The King significantly strengthened the city of Carcassonne, adding an inner ring-wall and making it an impregnable citadel. The fortresses of the Corbières were also considerably strengthened, so they became amongst the most formidable châteaux-forts in the whole of Medieval Europe.

However, the defeat of the 1240 rebellion did not put an end to insurrection. Only two years later, the Count of Toulouse himself declared war. He set up a vast coalition with two important enemies of the French monarchy, the Count of Marches and the King of England, Henry III. The counts of Cominges, Armagnac, Rodez and Foix also came on board, as did the Viscount of Narbonne, the exiled Trencavel and even the King of Aragon, soon joining the coalition.

A plan of campaign was carefully worked out. The King of England would land his troops at Royan, rallying to his side his vassals in Gascony. The Country of Toulouse, Béziers and Carcassonne would be mobilised to rise with the same energy. To give the starting signal of this imminent insurrection, Raymond VII could think of no more significant action than the assassination of those inquisitors stationed at Toulouse.

Raymond at first encountered some difficulty in enlisting support in carrying out this daring act, but he sent a emissary to the château of Montségur. From the time of the first invasion of 1209, Montségur had served as the main refuge for the senior Cathars of the Toulouse region, the very hierarchy of the Cathar church. At the instigation of Guilhabert de Castres, Montségur became the 'seat and capital' of the Cathar church. On the eve of Ascension Day 1242, a commando troop of fifty knights and sergeants came down from Montségur and arrived at Avignonet, where the tribunal of inquisitors was staying. The inquisitors and their followers, eleven people in all, were murdered with hatchets, while they slept.

News of the event spread fast. The people of Languedoc thought that the hour of their liberation had arrived. Insurrection broke out and quickly spread. The Count of Toulouse immediately went into action, but as he was entering Narbonne in triumph, he learned of the rout of the English army and the capitulation of the Count of Marches. The coalition had collapsed. The Count of Foix, ever the opportunist, seized the initiative and swapped sides, declaring war on Toulouse.

Montségur was to pay dearly for the assassinations of the Ascension 1242. The following spring, a huge army was assembled and the Cathar fortress was put to siege. This was a siege that was to last for ten months. Under the command of Pierre-Roger de Mirepoix, the garrison of Montségur fiercely defended the fortress and its population. Apart from the combatants, there were more than two hundred Perfecti, Parfaits and Parfaites, Bons-Hommes and Bonnes-Dames, plus a hundred or so followers of the Cathar church, women, old men and children, mostly relations of the Perfecti. The siege became untenable. Pierre-Roger submitted his terms of surrender on 2nd March 1244.

He obtained a truce for fifteen days. On Wednesday, 16th March he delivered up Montségur to the archbishop of Narbonne. When invited to abjure their faith, the Parfaits and Parfaites refused and were led that same day to the stake that had been hastily set up at the foot of the mountain. They numbered two hundred and twenty-five, two of them bishops. Among the executed were Raymond de Péreille's mother-in-law, a long-serving Parfait e, his wife Corba and his daughter Esclarmonde, both of whom had received Consolamentum on the eve of the surrender. The fall of Montségur did not sound the death knell of southern Catharism, far from it. Clandestine activity would last another seventy seven year. But the Church of the Bons-Hommes had lost its head and was no longer able to organise itself. It had survived the horrors of Crusade, but it would finally yield to the Inquisition.

b.   Cathar Castles

i.   MINERVE

Minerve was one of the major centres of Cathar activity.   A fortified village, built into the cleavage of a sheer limestone cliff, it became the refuge of many Perfecti trying to escape the wrath of the crusading troops, who by that time had sacked Béziers and other places around them with brutal ferocity. In 1210, Simon de Montfort's troops stood before Minerve. As in many sieges, the main concern of those besieged in the village was an adequate supply of fresh water, the one commodity that humans need in order to survive. At Minerve, the water was obtained from just one deep well, dug at the base of the cliff, the only access being a steep flight of fortified stairs. De Montfort's troops relentlessly pounded this stairway with their huge boulders, cast from large wooden catapults, a form of siege warfare tried and tested since early Roman times. Despite the ferocity of the pounding the crusaders imposed on this beautiful walled village, it took seven weeks to bring the villagers to their knees. Bombarded

Minerve where 180 'heretics' were burnt at the stake

relentlessly, scorched by the sun and deprived of water, the population had no choice but to surrender. Viscount William of Minerve negotiated the surrender and his life was spared, as were the lives of his soldiers. But he could not negotiate for the Cathar Perfecti, who were forced to choose between renouncing their beliefs and being burnt at the stake. There was only one answer:

"Neither death nor life shall tear us away from the faith we love."

On 22nd July 1210, one hundred and eighty Parfaits and Parfaites threw themselves onto the flames with great personal dignity and with their heads held high.

In more recent times, sculptor Jean-Luc Séverac, carved an unusual piece to commemorate the tragic sacrifice of the Perfecti burned at Minerve. Into a huge block of stone, he has carved the hollow form of a dove on the wing. This is not a sculpture of stone, but one of air, blue sky and exquisite landscape beyond. It is these natural aspects that give form and breath to this symbolic bird.

Also to be found in Minerve today is a most unusual museum, the Museum of Hurepel de Minerve. Taking the mythical life of Hurepel, a Cathar follower, a series of glass cases contain scenes from the Albigensian Crusade, particularly those incidents that took place in the surrounding district in the years 1209 and 1210. These scenes are exquisitely made, with miniature figures and authentic settings. These miniature tableaux tell the stories of the Crusade to powerful effect. Here we see the siege of Béziers, the massacre of its townspeople. Here we see Simon de Montfort usurping the title of the Viscount of Carcassonne. Here we see a miniature re-enactment of one of the most horrific incidents of the Crusade:

In the spring of 1210, Simon de Montfort laid siege to the quaint village of Bram, in the Plains of Lauragaise, between Carcassonne and Castelnaudry. After three days he launched a successful attack. Cathar Parfaits and Parfaites had lived openly in the village and this annoyed de Montfort. Consequently, he picked a hundred people at random, Cathars or not, and one by one they had their eyes gouged out, their noses and ears cut off, their lips cut back to expose their teeth. They were then tied together in a long pathetic convoy of pain and disfigurement. The first person, at the head of this tragic entourage, was allowed the luxury of keeping one eye to lead the rest on to Cabaret Castle and warn them there of what will happen if they support and shield Cathars.

That this horror was perpetrated merely as an example makes it all the more a crime against humanity. The fact that these scenes are constructed with small figures, miniatures with all the innocence of toy dolls, somehow seems to make such brutal events of the Crusade even more horrific. I do recommend a visit to the Musée Hurepel de Minerve. I have accompanied several groups of British young people, over in the Pyrénées region to climb mountains and canoe gorges, but also to find out about the Cathars who trod this land before them. I have always taken these young people to this splendid museum. They invariably say that it was one of the most interesting parts of their stay in France. I remember one occasion, when some of the group had gone on ahead, as young people often do, devouring the exhibition much quicker that those of us who take a more leisurely approach. Suddenly a big cheer came up from this group, as the neared the end of the exhibition. They had suddenly found out, from one of the glass case tableaux, that Simon de Montfort met his end at the hands of women! During the siege of Toulouse, the leader of the Crusade had his skull caved in with a rock flung from one of the huge catapults, the mangonel, used in siege warfare at that time. The mangonel used to defend Toulouse that had brought about the end of de Montfort was operated on that particular day by women.

ii.   TERMES

Raymond of Termes and his son, Olivier, had offered refuge to Cathars fleeing from the crusading armies. After Minerve, Simon de Montfort, taking heart from his victory moved directly to attack this imposing fortress, thought to be impregnable. It took a four month siege to dislodge this apparently impenetrable château and it was stoutly defended by Raymond of Termes. Huge mangonels were dragged with great effort from Carcassonne and were used to relentlessly pound the walls of the castle. But the summer sun shone fiercely down and, once more, the final defeat of a citadel defending the Cathars was due to a shortage of drinking water. The emptied water tanks, not the ferocity of the attack, was what forced Raymond to surrender. The relieved crusaders advanced to take possession of the castle, but were met with a hail of arrows from archers placed all along the battlements. Termes was not quite ready to throw in the towel just yet. That night, a severe storm replenished the water butts and the resistance stood firm a little longer. One night, a strange commotion gripped the castle. Some of the men defending it were trying to slip away unnoticed. But the alarm was raised and

they were massacred by crusaders. When dysentery started to wreak havoc amongst those remaining, Raymond of Termes felt that his men were too weak to repel the assailants. He finally gave in and the castle was taken.

This is a place of poignant loneliness. Wild, lost in desolate scenery, nearly at the centre of a large rocky labyrinth, which spreads from the valley of the river Aude to the Mediterranean Sea. All that remains of Termes now are extensive ruins, the most striking feature being a façade complete with an unusual cross-shaped window. This window seems to be stencilled against the blue sky and green fields beyond and ironically recalls all the bloody struggles that ensued in this region in which the Catholics and the Cathars were engaged - ironic because the only thing that divided these two opposing forces was their interpretation of Christ's message.

iii.   PUIVERT

Puivert Castle owes much of its reputation to its association with the troubadours and the 'courts of love'. The troubadours used their talents to celebrate a certain romantic way of life and Puivert Castle became famous as a major meeting place for poets and musicians. In the parts of the castle ruins still intact, the great hall, used as a musicians' chamber, can be visited. Stanchions supporting the ribbed vaulted roof have corbels on top, each with carvings of musicians, playing lute, saqueboute and vielle'roue, the distinct sounding hurdy-gurdy. The art form of the troubadours was highly prized by noble ladies of the day. Puivert is a very well-preserved château, with ongoing renovation work. It dominates the green valley below, from atop its high peak, with a distinctive gateway and a square keep standing above its long ramparts. There is a strong sense of atmosphere at Puivert and it is easy to imagine the festivities and musical soirées that must have taken place here. When de Montfort's forces laid siege during the autumn of 1210, these gentlefolk surrendered within three days. In the village of Puivert, just below the castle, there is an extremely informative museum, the Quercorb Museum. As well as fascinating moving tableaux depicting life and trades in Cathar times, there is also a scale model of the castle, illustrating how the missing sections might have looked in the overall construction. The most splendid display, however, is a room containing accurate reproductions of the musical instruments used in the 13th century. They are exhibited in a glass case at the centre of a darkened room, with reproductions of the sculpted musicians from Puivert castle on the walls around them, individually spotlighted. Music of the period plays throughout the day and the whole effect is very pleasing, making Puivert one of the most satisfying of all the castles to visit.

iv.   LASTOURS

After the fall of Minerve, Termes, and Puivert, not to mention the cruel sacking of Béziers and the tragic fall of Carcassonne, the Lord of Lastours, Pierre Roger de Cabaret, put up stern resistance to the crusading armies. He was, with Trencavel, one of the guardians of Carcassonne. After the fall of the city he took retreat to his fortresses, high above the Orbiel and Grésilhou valleys. The four castles of Lastours sit high and proud, each on its own rocky perch, within close proximity. A rock wall, 1,300 feet long and 165 feet wide, outlines a site so outstanding and strategically important it has been occupied since prehistoric times. At the time of the Albigensian Crusade, there may only have been three fortresses, since the Régine Tower, the smallest of the four, was probably built by the king's men, probably in about 1260. However, the monumental concept and effort employed to erect three or four sister fortresses on such a site is astounding, to say the least. The highest point of the site is occupied by the Fleur-Espine Castle, meaning 'Thornflower'. Further down, and somewhat

Puivert Castle

isolated from the others, is Quertinheux Castle. This consists principally of a round tower, surrounded by an elaborate series of massive walls. Even in its ruined state, it has all the features of a stalwart medieval fortified castle. The largest and most famous of the castles is Cabaret. The local lords took their name from it and the name of Cabaret came to symbolise the resistance mounted against the Crusade. On the face of it, de Montfort might have expected a real struggle here, involving, as it did, simultaneous attack on three fortresses, well protected by the size and sheerness of their location, totally inaccessible to the vast war machines. Sensing a possible defeat, de Montfort hatched his cruel plan to send in the one hundred grossly disfigured captives from the village of Bram, eyes gouged out, noses, ears and lips cut off, tied together and led by the one-eyed guide. Even this extreme atrocity at first failed to have its desired effect, but when the Lord of Cabaret heard of the fall of Termes, thought to be impregnable, he negotiated a surrender and the château of Lastours fell into de Montfort's hands, without the bitter struggle he had been anticipating. However, Pierre Roger de Cabaret did not stop fighting. He recaptured the castles when de Montfort was occupied elsewhere and they became the refuge of a large Cathar community. The vast caves under Quertinheux were probably used for Cathar ceremonies and there is even a local legend that subterranean passages ran from here all the way to Carcassonne. Unlikely, but a strong spiritual conception. By the year 1224, Cabaret was the seat of the Cathar diocese of Carcasse. The castles fell into royal hands during the second Crusade, under Louis VIII, with several of the nobles of Cabaret taking Consolamentum.

Two views of Peyrepertuse, the pierced rock, a veritable 'Celestial Carcassonne'

v.   PEYREPERTUSE

This is the fortress with the outline of a ship, as if washed onto the top of its Corbières mountain range by the storms of history. Its unusual name is derived from petra pertusa, meaning the 'pierced rock', taken from the huge fissure in the mountain. The approach to Peyrepertuse, high above the village of Duilhac, reveals what seems to be, at first sight, a sheer-sided mountain. But it slowly becomes clear that on top there really is a castle, a vast fortress, virtually containing a small Medieval town; the 'Celestial Carcassonne', largest of all the Cathar Castles.

The castle appears at first to be inaccessible. The assent is via a narrow, shady path, always with a delicate scent of box-wood, which leads direct to the barbican, or gate-tower. The curtain-walls of the castle run the length of the sheer face of the mountain. One can only wonder at the grim determination it took to build this vast structure in such an inaccessible place.

Once inside, one is confronted by a maze of walls, structures and buildings. The whole place has stood up well to the ravages of time and it is possible to feel the solid, secure grandeur that was once Peyrepertuse. Haughty, silent and out of reach, it exudes and sense of pride, which no doubt symbolizes that which was felt by the defending knights, in those far off Middle Ages. To say nothing of the spectacular views from all sides of its high walls.

Peyrepertuse Castle probably dates back to the 9th century, but by the year 1111 it was owned by the Count of Barcelona, later falling into the hands of the King of Aragon and then into the ownership of Guillaume de Peyrepertuse. During the Albigensian Crusade, Guillaume surrendered first to Simon de Montfort, in 1217. But it was regained, along with Puilaurens Castle, when Guillaume joined forces with Trencavel. In 1240 the castle was under siege by Jean de Beaumont, forcing Guillaume once more to surrender. The mighty fortress of Peyrepertuse now belonged to the King of France, Saint Louis, and he carried out extensive renovations, making it the most impressive fortress in the Pyrénées.

vi.   PUILAURENS

On the border of Languedoc and French Catalonia, Puilaurens sits high above the picturesque village of Lapradelle, some of the most romantic ruins of the region. The way into Puilaurens Castle is curious, in that it follows a long path through the depths of a rock fold, with an endless succession of crossed-walls as obstacles, bad enough for modern day tourists, but a formidable military problem to invading forces. Isolated at the top of its hill, Puilaurens is an amazingly well-preserved piece of fortress architecture. It resembles an impressive stone crown, perched on top of a sheer spur of rock, and is consequently known locally as the 'Cathar Crown'. Some of the original 11th century structure is still intact, but much of the labyrinth of rooms and passages date from 12th and 13th centuries. In the latter century it belonged to the Lords of

Fenouillet and later, Guillaume de Peyrepertuse. The castle resisted numerous attacks, by Simon de Montfort and his successors, until the end of the Crusade. Many Cathar deacons sought refuge in Puilaurens after the fall of Montségur. It is thought that the castle finally surrendered around 1256, possibly at the same time as Quéribus.

I have slept in Puilaurens, with a group of friends, and I can report that strong local rumours of a strange white lady who perennially haunts the château did not manifest themselves. At least, not that night!

vii.   QUÉRIBUS

From the 'Celestial Carcassonne' of Peyrepertuse, looking across the valley to the mountains opposite, the most imposing sight is the château of Quéribus, standing foursquare atop a striking rocky crag, a high peak of naked limestone. From a closer viewpoint, it appears as if the citadel has been carved out of the rock, could it be by some particularly bold giant? The road up to it is interminable, spiralling round the crag on which the castle sits, giving breathtaking views of the valley below. The view from its ramparts is astonishing, seeming to last forever, without crag or mountain to interrupt the panorama. A watchman placed here on a clear day could almost see the ebb and flow of the Mediterranean.

The magnificent Quéribus

Quéribus really is magnificent. The château is a most impressive structure, the stock, square, dominant keep being a prominent feature of the landscape for miles around. The structure itself almost exudes a pride in its heroic place in history. At least, that is what the guidebooks say. For Quéribus was the very last bastion of Cathar resistance to the Crusade, finally surrendering in 1256.

In fact, Quéribus withstood a long and vicious siege by the royal vassal based in Carcassonne, but the lord of the region, Chabert de Barbeira, was defeated in battle, having fallen in an ambush, and he negotiated his freedom against the surrender of both Quéribus and Puilaurens. Hereafter the Cathar followers were compelled to go into hiding, devoid of all political and military backing.

Royal garrisons were maintained here, at Quéribus, in Puilaurens and in Peyrepertuse, even beyond 1658, when the Roussillon was annexed to France, making these fortresses of far less strategic importance.

viii.   ARQUES

At Arques, on a long and winding road from Quillan to Narbonne, there was a small fortress at the time of the Crusade, but not the one illustrated here. Unique in the region, the siting of the fortress was not atop a mountain peak, but set firmly at the same level to the village of the same name nearby. Following the destruction of Arques village and the old castle by the crusading forces, Simon de Montfort gave the land to his friend, Pierre de Voisin, who rebuilt part of the château, the impressive square keep, which makes it such a distinctive and imposing fortress, being added by his descendants at the end of the 14th century. According to surviving records of the Papal inquisitor Jacques Fournier, around 1300, Arques still had a few Cathars amongst its population. Arques is also best remembered as the home of Déodat Roché, writer on Catharism, poet and co-founder, with his friend René Nelli, of 'Cahiers d'études cathares'. He was born there in 1877 and died there in 1978, living for the latter years of his life in the château itself. There is now a museum dedicated to his work in the village.

ix.   ROQUEFIXADE

Five miles west of Lavalet, the remains of Roquefixade castle are on top of a limestone peak, deeply hewn by erosion. A narrow path leads from the village below to the foot of the rocky crag, then climbs steeply round the Northwest face of the cliff. In fact, Roquefixade Castle is virtually inaccessible from the village and almost indistinguishable on the skyline.

Roquefixade: almost imperceptible from the road

You really do have to look. But then you see it, strategically important, overlooking the plains beyond. Close up, the ruins are more impressive, particularly an imposing part of the wall, borne by a vault spanning the slit in the cliff.

The name comes from roca fisada, the rocky cleft in which the castle has been built, filled in by the construction of an arch, supported by ramparts. The castle was a secure refuge for the local people during the Albigensian Crusade and never fell to the crusaders. It is thought that the inhabitants of the castle communicated with the castle of Montségur, across the valley, by lighting huge bonfires. One of the few times in the Crusade when fire was used peacefully!

x.   MONTSÉGUR

Montségur is a special place indeed. Set on its particularly distinctive pog, it is the 'Glastonbury Tor' of the Languedoc. And like Glastonbury, Montségur is gradually acquiring a similar legendary status. Not only are tourists attracted here, in vast droves, but also poets, artists, mystics, photographers, seekers after truth and enlightenment.

Montségur is the symbol of Catharism, par excellence. Its mythical status relies not only on the martyrs of the flames, the two hundred and twenty-five Parfaits and Parfaites burned at the foot of the hill in March 1244, but also on the four Cathar supporters, who escaped down the backside of the mountain the evening before the mass burning, carrying with them the most important Cathar secrets. Whether this was secret knowledge, mystical documents, valuable treasure or even the Holy Grail itself, is a riddle now located in the mists of time.

The climb up to Montségur is almost a religious experience. You arrive at the top, breathless, yet fulfilled. The views are breathtaking, the castle itself impressive in stature and with an overwhelming sense of spirit.

The memorial to the 225 Cathars massacred at Montségur

The siege of Montségur was the making of the myth. Eight months of struggle and resistance that have come to symbolise not only the Cathar courage and endurance, but also.... During May 1243, some 6,000 men led by the Seneschal of Carcassonne, Hugues des Arcis, and the Archbishop of Narbonne, Pierre Amiel, took up position at the foot of Montségur. There was a grotesque imbalance of forces.

The total number of people living in the castle was around five hundred, with a garrison of about a hundred and fifty, with fifteen knights and squires. The crusaders probably anticipated a short siege, as most of the surrounding castles had surrendered relatively speedily, usually for lack of water. At Montségur the problem was quite different. The particular shape of the pog (derived from an Occitanian word, 'ueg' or puog', meaning mount, hill or peak) made it difficult for the sieging army, which required a large body of soldiers to overcome the lie of the land.

Try as they might to stop them, messages, supplies and reinforcements got through the besiegers' ranks. Weeks passed and became months. Winter was drawing close. The crusaders began to lose patience. Hugues des Arcis took on Gascon mercenaries, who knew the terrain. They advanced by night, killed the first defenders they encountered and seized the tower at the Eastern end of the pog. With this advantage, crusaders were able to set up catapults and the pounding of the ramparts began. The siege went on through January and February of 1244. But food was running short, the winter was severe, despair was setting in and surrender was negotiated.

Surrender terms were relatively mild. Pierre Roger de Mirepoix, commander of the garrison in Montségur, and Hugues des Arcis, heading up the crusading forces, agreed terms:

> The defenders had a truce of fifteen days, during which time they could stay in the fortress and then hand it over to the King of France.

> Convictions against a number of defenders were to be waived.

> Defending soldiers would be freed after appearing before the Inquisition.

> Any other person living in the castle would also be free, if they gave up and renounced the Cathar faith, after making a statement to the Inquisition.

> The rest would be burnt at the stake.

There are a number of theories why the defending forces asked for a truce of fifteen days. Perhaps Pierre Roger de Mirepoix was expecting some reinforcements. Possibly the defenders needed to put their affairs in order. It is known that the Cathar Perfecti used the truce to prepare themselves spiritually for death. They gave all their worldly possessions to the soldiers who had so stoutly defended them for ten months. Some soldiers and other people actually converted to Catharism, even knowing that this meant going to a certain death in the flames.

On 16 March 1244 the surrender was affected. The archbishop of Narbonne and the Seneschal of Carcassonne waited to take possession of the castle. Pierre Roger de Mirepoix handed over the castle. The Cathars, led by Bertrand Marty, their Bishop, walked down the mountain. At the bottom, there was an enclosure stacked high with firewood, which was lit as they approached.

Not a single Cathar chose to recant his or her faith. Climbing ladders up the side of the blazing enclosure, the Perfecti threw themselves into the flames. Husbands and wives hand in hand, noblemen, merchants, the injured carried into the flames on their stretchers, civilians, and soldiers, all were united in their faith and in their act of martyrdom.

Not all the Cathars were burnt that day. At the request of Bernard Marty, four Cathars had been lowered over the back of the castle and down the cliff by rope on the evening before the surrender. They made their way to a cave, on the other side, where they recovered some particular things left by other Cathars the previous Christmas. They then made their way to the castle of Usson, after which all trace of them disappears. What did they take with them out of Montségur the night before the martyrs were burned? Treasure? Probably not. They were breaking the terms of surrender, by this action, against all their moral integrity. The action would also have put Pierre Roger de Mirepoix into a great deal of trouble, if it had been discovered, and the mild terms negotiated for the defending forces would certainly have been put in jeopardy. From this point of view, hiding treasure could not have been the sole purpose of their quest. We do not have any definite answer to the mystery of what they did rescue that night, but this all adds to the charm of mythical Montségur.

Perhaps the real treasure of Montségur can be found in the numbers of Cathar supporters who took Consolamentum just before they marched down the hill into the flames. These people could easily have saved their lives, yet they chose to go to a painful death, alongside those Good People with whom they had just shared the last ten months of their lives. This speaks volumes for the integrity of Catharism.

It fills me with admiration, for sure!

Chapter 15
SPECTACLE SON & LUMIÉRE - 'LES CATHARES . . . .'

As performed in the Pyrénées village of Caudiès-de-Fenouillèdes

The following script was given to me, as a present, by George Vayre, from the small village of Caudiès, set in the valley between the Corbières and the Fenouillèdes mountains, close to the former Cathar stronghold of Puilaurens. George Vayre was a most respected man in the community, a true man of the Languedoc, whose wise counsel was much sought after, a source of help, solace and advice. He died in 1994, after a particularly fulfilled life. The script is one of the best presents I have ever had.

This son et lumiére production was performed by the community of Caudiès in 1972. The passage of time, since the incidents depicted in the script took place here, some eight hundred years, has not in any way dented the passion for the land of Occitan, the respect for the Cathar tradition, and the resentment of what the invading forces from the North inflicted on this region. This document is so powerful in expression, so evocative in description and so sincere in its spiritual qualities that it is presented in its entirety. It appears in English for the first time:

'THE CATHARS . . .'

I have raised my arms to the Very High One
And His lightning has ravished me to the seventh heaven.

I have called upon fire for deliverance
And my joy has been exalted in the pain of the pyre at the stake.

I give the soiled clothing of my flesh in offering to the flames.

Fire who is light and rips through the appearance of being
To reveal the splendour within
In the unfathomable giddiness of your flames
And the ultimate agony which was the innate call of my life
My soul finds the end of a long exile.

No pain compares to this supreme gift
A surrender bestowing upon me the light of the essential world.

You are the disembodied flesh who frees the body
Fire who dissolves the darkness
Multiple body around a single core
Fire who is strength and salvation
Who frees me from the clutches of the earth.

You are a surge, a call, and you shed through me new blood
In the cruel voluptuousness of your embrace
My soul thrills as your flame skims over it
Then leaps forward with greater abandon.

You are a blinding dawn
In your intimacy we find the bounty of the sun
Your shimmering tongue swallowing the energies of the dark.

New life revealed in the trial of agony
Life arising from matter returned to the void
Fire who is birth and within whom death discards and annihilates itself.

At the end of our night
Lightning has surged in the thundering
Of a world open to the glory of the Very High One
My eyes are enlightened to the ultimate vision of the spirit of the eternal world New
sky and new earth
Created before the beginning of times
And that centuries upon centuries cannot yet repeal.

Blessed be the fire of deliverance, blessed be the fire, conqueror of death . . .

May the breath of the heavens guide hence our souls to the throne of God . .

I remember a country as slow as a breath of Autumn air
As blue as twilight
A country open to the silence of unknown parts.

I remember a land with a deep and gorgeous belly
Which the sea covers with a sunny tan

Fixed anchors at the foot of pearly cliffs
Far away sails
Ships wallowing in the heavy seas . . .

Can I recall a greater calamity?

Those days were made of space and blue sky
Those days were yielded to ever new Springs
To quivering harvests
To the whiff of Autumn . . .
Reeds, tamarinds, pink laurel and the frozen movement of the striding hills
I remember snow splashed with sunlight.

But who will tell today of the grief of my Occitanian lands?

I remember glowing dawns
Opulent cities around austere cathedrals
Towers tearing the clouds apart
Banners vibrant with purple and gold
Battlement walls mighty as mountains, more sombre than a storm.

I cannot recall more cruel a storm . . .

I remember a country tinged with blue
A people with hands as rugged as the stones found in a ravine
Their eyes stroked the mountains and filled with the dream of an intimate sea
Their skin, torn from the very hues of the earth, amazed even the sun
The wind made them stronger than trees
O loyal and generous people . . .

Today, their roots bleed, ripped clear from their soil
And fear sends a shiver through our hands

In this land which knew neither wolves nor vultures
Where the grass echoed with the calls of Spring
These men were pure and peaceful.

They knew to listen in the night
When darkness whispers
When stones hug the last warm sparks of sunlight

When a shadow glides over the rounded head of the forsaken ears of corn When
pine trees tirelessly create the call of lost horizons . . .

These men were the very gift of their land

But what despairing night has killed their memory?

I remember a language redolent of the burning arid breath of middays
Harsh and pungent like the bushes of the heath
A language endowed with the curving grace and suspended leap of a wave
Blue as a light August night scented with sweet heather
A language with the clarity of mimosa in winter
As lively as the almond tree in January
More coloured, more white than an iris
My language of Oc which brought together the deep voice of the billowing sea
And the sharp cries of the wind in the hills
Crying out the name of beloved lands . . .

My voice of Oc dying
In a slit throat

THE SONG OF LANGUEDOC

Where did they come from?
From which pure source did these men stream through our country?

They came in an evening of torment and peace
They descended and dwelt within us
Their faces etched deep like the many paths they have trod
So many nights of vigil burned in their eyes
So many foreign winds had worn their hands . . .
But so much goodness lit up their eyes that only one word rose to our lips
To call them: they were the 'Good Men'

Apostles of time without bounds they dwelt in one huge prayer
Gathering a sublime strength from their exhausted bodies
The word of God guided their steps like a living light
Their hands were open to the poor
At cross-roads they erected crosses to show us the way

Crosses that shone brighter than those in our churches
In the evening their voice would fill our market places
And our towns would lie peaceful in the passion of their words
Old people felt the flow of new life in their frozen limbs
No one could resist their call
For never did the stones of our churches hear more saintly prayers
A heavenly breath spread in the plains and hills
And lit up the very hearts in our breasts

The twilight mists were clearing
And the assembled crowds called the Spirit of God upon themselves
With deep fervour
Prophets whose bodies were more mournful than ashes
Scornful of rich dwellings and human honours
Taking shelter in the heart of the mountains
They lived on the bounteous rhythm of the promise of eternal life

Born of the dawn upon our fields of midday upon our roads
They opened in their wake celestial paths
Fresher than the newest morning light
Their word will echo through our towns forever
A voice which filled the skies
Weaving a powerful invocation of a people lifted out of misery
And raised to the delights of the river of life . . .

BROTHER IS SPIRIT

Brother is Spirit, the time is near when God, manifesting His Almightiness, will throw Satan back into the void, that angel of darkness and evil principle of our world.

Let then all which is matter go back to the void and let the Spirit triumphant rise to the Heavens, its one and only home.

Woe unto him who welcomes the forces of evil by clinging to the goods of this world. Let all flesh, impure in its very origin, be so loathsome that it be reduced to ashes, to be offered to death through fasting and mortifying, and that thus, the soul carrying the spirit be freed.

Banish forever from your hearts all attempts to love this world: for these meadows, these forests, these dwellings, all wealth, the flesh itself of your bodies are but vanity and the impure seduction, which the celestial fire will consume and reduce to the original state of void.

This world you inhabit is not the work of God, but of Satan, Prince of Darkness. For our misfortune, he has buried us in this contemptible body. Shame on those who will honour all creation . . . For here is what was revealed by Jesus, Son of God, to the apostle John:

"I, John, your brother who suffers the same tribulations to attain the Kingdom of the Heavens, as I rested upon the breast of Our Lord Jesus Christ, I told him: 'Lord, before the fall of Satan, in which state of glory was he with your Father?'

And he answered me: 'He was in such exalted glory that he ruled over all the virtues of the Heavens . . . But he proposed to place his throne above the Heavens themselves, as he longed to be like the Very High One himself . . . And thus he ensconced himself upon the Heavens . . . And he took the crown of the angel ruling over the waters: of one half he made the light of the moon; of the other, the light of the stars. With precious stones, he created all the legions of the stars . . . And he made the thunder, rains, hail and snow. And he installed his angels to rule over them. And he ordered the Earth to produce all the animals, reptiles, trees and grasses; and he ordered the sea to produce fishes and the air to produce the birds in the sky. After which he mused awhile and then made man so he would be his own slave or the slave of his own nature. And he ordered the angel of the third heaven to enter his body of mud from which he then took a piece to make of it another body in the shape of woman. And he ordered the angel of the second heaven to enter the body of the woman. But these angels burst into tears when they saw that they were trapped in mortal shapes and that they had become unlike themselves in those shapes; and Sathanas directed them to commit the act of flesh in their bodies of mud; and they did not understand that they were thus guilty of sin . . .   And then did the reign of Satan come about in this world . . .'"

From now hence, let the purest amongst you retire from the world and give themselves over to the contemplation of the Spirit. They will receive the consolation reserved for the true servants of God and will be called 'Perfecti'.

WORDS OF QUARREL AND OF HATRED

See now from then on that this country is struck in its very depths by an illness that sword, hatred and greed will worsen until the death of a loyal and generous people, cut by a thousand unfair wounds.

From the very places where peace and the supreme love of a God of goodness flowered, in the name of the holy cross, symbol of suffering offered for the salvation of man, discord gives right to violence and the lure of fatal death.

Hear ye rise beneath the vault of our churches words of quarrel and of hatred:

"Brothers who yield in all humility to the authority of Christ and of his minister in the Church, our Pope, successor of Peter the Apostle, a cruel evil has taken hold of our people; their heretical vermin has infected our roads, plains, hills and public squares. Do not allow this evil to take root and spread around you, on you or in you. If one of those scoundrels finds himself on your path, set your most ferocious dog on him and do not have any rest until the wretch has been torn apart and thrown dead in the pool of his own impure blood.

For those of that breed - may the shame and malediction be forever upon them - professes two gods or two lords, one good the other evil; they maintain that the creation of all things visible and embodied is not the work of God, Heavenly Father, but of the devil or Satan, whom they call the evil god. Thus, they make out two creations, that of the invisible and disembodied things, and that of the visible and embodied things. Further more, they refuse baptism by water and all the sacraments of our church, they evade all the rituals and do not recognise the presence of Christ in the holy species.

They hold that only their church is the church of Christ; as to our church, they dare to call it the mother of fornication, the great Babylon, the basilica or synagogue of Satan . . .

God orders, through the voice of our Holy Father and that of our revered bishops, that all Christians should hunt down those impudent people.

You will recognise those priests who are called 'Perfecti' from several signs: They live in the greatest destitution and refuse any goods from this world.

They fast three Lents per year with only bread and water.

They never eat any meat, do not even touch it, nor cheese, nor eggs, nor anything that is born of flesh, through reproduction.

They would, under no circumstances, kill animals or birds, as they hold and believe that non-sentient beings are receptacles of the souls that leave the bodies of men, when they have not been accepted into their sect and order, through the laying on of hands, according to their rites, and that these souls transmigrate from one body to any other.

They deny women and condemn all procreation as a crime against the Spirit.

Because of them, calamity has descended on our lands and misery upon these people, who gave in to these infernal beliefs.

Let us erect tremendous pyres at the top of our hills and in front of our churches, for the destruction of this malevolent breed, the opprobrium of our Holy Church.

Let the winds disperse the ashes of their impure bodies, as far as can be, from a country which casts them away.

Be they brother, father, friend or elder, let no sacrilegious feeling of pity spare these impious ones and let our country recover its former peace and abundance in its obedience to our Lord God."

SONG OF THE PERSECUTED

A multitude of innocents will then die
For one man struck to death
A multitude will perish by fire and sword
Through the atrocities of the barbaric crusaders from the North
For one man Pierre de Castlenau
Invested of the full power of the Roman church
And obsessed with ferreting out heretics
Was assassinated on his way to Rome

It is now a country in mourning
Where the cypress no longer yields to the wind

In the solitude of barren lands

It is the toll of a country
Sounding the bitter complaint of the birds of darkness
On the desolate rocks

It is the toll of a country in tears
Where the trees refuse to feed on a beloved blood
Where dilapidated battlement walls now give way to brambles

The pain-filled raven shrouds under his black wing
The parting of our Occitan land

Sword fire and blood . . .
Hell hath no greater fury

The morning winds bring the rumble of gallops and heavy armour
What is this reddish cloud
Projecting upon our houses the red shadow of a cross?
Strange birds have coloured our hills
The frightening lark has risen high in the sky
So high that no black flyer can reach it

A shout has sounded beyond the clouds
At the heart of the sun
Where it now dwells

Who hasn't heard in the muggy night
Our walls cracking and shadows groaning?
The flowers of the orchard withered on the branch
The willow has ripped its entrails with darkness . . .

Strange rumours are perceived in our step
On ground greyer than ashes
Can they be the sound of a calamity never heard before?

This land is open from now on
To the steel and greed of the French . . .

Dismal crusade where the cross bleeds like a sword

Did God command this gathering of soldiers
So keen to inflict suffering and death?

Is he a just God who dwells in churches
Sheltering crime and perjury?

These massacres
These pyres
The pillage of our wealth
Are they from the will of a benevolent God?

Is it in his all powerful name that our walls
Our doors and our fields are surrendered
To the lust and barbarism of a foreign army?

Of our blue seasons
Of our dwellings opened in peace to the road
Of our fecund plains
Of our walls rooted in our mountains
Nothing is left but ruins
Grief and desolation . . .

It is a deafening death rattle
From a land where generosity made her a prey to death

Today they gave onto the flames an entire town:

    Béziers
    Tongues of fire
    Higher than the towers of our strongholds
    Rose into the sky
    Carrying the cry of people
    Thrown into the tortures of hell

Everything speaks of dying screams
Maddened looks in children's eyes
Cowering in arms unable to ward off oncoming death

All tells of the enraged French drunk on violence

Today a shroud of savagery weighs down the land
And I have no more tears to give

Today death made its imprint in the Corbiéres:

> Carcassonne
> Minerve
> Termes
> You surrendered strongholds
> I pity your useless walls

Today Raymond-Roger
 Viscount of Carcassonne
Gave his last breath in the shameful night of a dungeon
His eyes robbed of the light of this earth
Will open in the splendour of the eternal Throne

Today the sky darkened
For death
In the guise of a glint of steel
Had fallen upon Lavaur
            The stones of its walls came down in the delirium of dust . . .

Today Dame Guiralde was given to the barbarism of the crusade
Publicly raped and thrown alive down a well
Then they buried her under huge boulders

Woe unto those who killed her
For Dame Guiralde was saintly and charitable
And carried in her breast the fruit of a generous love

Today our disembowelled lands
Our land ripped apart by the tumult of battle
By the trampling of armies
            Our exhausted land is dying

And its body only burns
Grief and barrenness
There is no more refuge for our people

Death is a traveller with a hundred faces
  At the road crossings
    Behind the battlements of our cities
    At the heart of our homes
She is a shadow
Cruel and without mercy

Day after day they have killed
Burned and seeded the pale crops of the dead
Grief follows in their steps
Clouds of ashes swirl around their armies
And no one dares look upwards to the sky

Upon their breast the crosses shone like blood
And their heart poured out words of hatred . . .
    Oh! the disgrace of those troops
    Feasting at the foot of towns in mourning . . .

Our hills have burst into flames with these pyres from hell
Flames feeding on our flesh and blood . . .
    Bodies thrown into such an odious death
    Which familiar place will now welcome your graves?

Occitan country
Chains of blood
Weigh from now to Eternity
On your bruised flesh

The roads of our Corbières
Will never cease to remember this crowd
Of unfortunate people
To whom the mad crusaders had slashed the eyes
And who were prodded on and on
By some knight of Satan

Bleeding shadows
Wandering already in the dusk of your death
Calling on it as a liberation
Through the swords of the victors
Or under their horses hooves

Times are no more for songs of love or fieldwork
Today the only talk is of injustice
And the crimes of a church
Which no one can claim as his

SONG OF THE TROUBADOUR

The song of the troubadour has the roughness
Of a shout too long suspended:

> *"No kind of fear will prevent me from writing a pamphlet*
> *Of the intention of those clerics full of falsehood*
> *So that the felony and trickery of a clergy full of lies*
> *Be known everywhere*
> *For the more strength and power are given to it*
> *The greater are the evil deeds it performs*
>
> *In truth our pastors have become as stealing wolves*
> *They steal on all sides under pretext of bringing*
> *Peace and sweet comfort to their flocks*
> *Then when they have reduced them to submission*
> *They strike them dead or exile them*
> *Those false pastors so hard-hearted I despise of them*
>
> *Then they also bring shame upon their century*
> *And upon God on high*
> *For they have wallowed today in the bed of a woman*
> *Tomorrow still reeking of this sin*
> *They will hold in their hands the body of Our Lord*
> *Here is truly a heresy deserving of death*
> *For no priest sullied in the bed of a prostitute*
> *Should hold the next day the body of God*
>
> *And if you dare to clamour against them*
> *It is they who will accuse you*
> *They who will excommunicate you*
> *If you give them your wealth*
> *They will return neither support nor friendship*

Holy Mary
Our Lady of Grace
Give me to see the day when I will be able to resist them
And feel less dread

Go pamphlet!
Go your way and take care of this elegy of falsehood
For whomsoever falls into their hands
Is as good as dead . . .

In Toulouse they know how true this is
These words I speak . . . "

Land of Occitania torn from the hands of those who love you most
What foreign face has pain etched into your flesh?

Our plains where softly lay the ample wave of crops
Now dried up black and sterile
The trees along the paths only wear on their bruised arms
The absence of Spring
The shiny broom tree loses its glow
At the edge of our province
Mutilated bodies
Abandoned to the elements on the side of the road
On a forgetful soil
Dead bodies that no land will welcome any more . . .

Oh! the repulsive epic of those who took our goods and our lives
Simon de Montfort which prayer awaits on your heart
At the end of your relentless violence?
Is he a God of goodness
He that your soul turns to
In the solitude of your meditations?
And how can so much cruelty lay hidden
Behind the cross on your chest?
You carry through your armies
The taste for the blood awash on your standards
And the ferocity of the lion decorating your coat of arms
You know the wiles
The harshness of battle

The breaten of cavalry charges
The intoxication of meeting out death
You know the quiver of the hand
Plunging a sword through the throat of an enemy
The contained madness of horses
The bitter smell of victories . . .

Have you ever dreamt of happy times
Far from the tumult of battle?
        Blessed be the stone
        Which one day will smash your face in . . .

Valiant Toulouse succumbs today
In the last start of its assembled forces
In vain our prayers and travail have been
Since today death strangles our stronghold
Yet no one here can be accused of impiety
No one has harmed the honour of Christ or his church
And if the walls protect men guilty of heresy
They are above all our brothers
And no duty would force us to betray them
Or cart them away from us

Toulouse dies today as dies its mother land of Oc

This country was made of blue at dawn
And my hands now clutch my pain
Under each stone lies a grave
Walls knocked down
Houses burnt to a cinder
Land without memory . . .

Who will now recall the voice of the winds
In the still swinging of pines?
Night without end
Thick silence in empty space
What remaining heart yet beats in these places
Only visited now by the breath of the heavens?

Montségur
You who signals on the slopes of a mountain

The way towards a purer life
Refuge and sanctuary
Whose walls stretch towards the sky
As do the hearts of those sheltering within them

Stronghold
Securing a treasure of such wealth
That man's greed will never possess it

Montségur
Who guards the heart of your fortress
The glow of a nearby heaven . . .
May God's wrath forever descend on those who treacherously
Penetrated your venerated sanctum

Through the ravines
Stone by stone
Bush by bush
The saintly group walks towards the stake
Their song of rejoicing and their resolute faces
Tell me how much those martyrs
Were deserving of a better life

Through the flames of the pyre
Peace on those innocent souls
The eternal spirit radiates
May they never be forgotten in God's love

        Montségur, holy mountain . . .

Land of Occitania
You whose wound rips through time itself
Turn finally your eyes towards the rocks of Fenouillèdes
Where lie ensconced the last defenders of our stolen nation

        Peyrepertuse
        Aguilar
        Puilaurens
        All strongholds soon surrendered
        To the unfounded pretensions of foreign lords
        All have foundered

Alone Quéribus
Still defies the violence of the crusaders
Insolent rock on the border of Languedoc
In its centre coincide all solstice celebrations
Born of the single-mindedness of a people . . .

Immune stone
Erected towards realms
Both huge
Unknown and promised
Superhuman achievement
Born of the faith of men
Set on refusing to submit . . .

Quéribus
From the top of which one discovers
The sea reflecting its immutable solitude
From which the oaks of the Corbiéres
Receive life and light
Last stand ramparts
Breaking the oncoming tide
Stronghold in the sky
You would still enjoy a free life
If it wasn't for the wiles of Olivier de Termes
Neighbouring lord
Who had the better of your tall walls
Surrendered even before having engaged battle . . .

Where are the last 'Good Men'?
Disappeared in the night of an inglorious defeat?

For a sun and a ground ripped asunder
For forgetting borders
For so many horizons beyond seeing
For a common prayer and the expectation of a common salvation
For the light of midday and the denial of barren nights
This land carries the wounded stigma of our memories . . .

There remains today
Beyond death and time's forgetfulness
Names ringing out with pain:

Montségur
Minerve
Peyrepertuse
Puilaurens
Quéribus
and those words saved from darkness

"We have called upon deliverance by fire
And all your joy was exalted in the torment at the stake"

I have cast away the impure clothing of my flesh
To offer myself to the delirium of the flames
My soul quivers in the embrace of the fire caressing it
And abandons it to renewed light

Fire
Your many arms draw
The offerings of the sun
Unbearable voluptuousness
Agonising and intoxicating intimacy
With the essential world
At the end of our night
I call upon the bolt of lightning . . .

The breath of the heavens guides our souls . . .

Oh! the splendours of divine space . . .
Spirit . . .
Eternity . . .
Unknown earth and sky . . .
Whiteness of dawn . . .
Time before the beginning of times . . .
Spirit . . .

Caudiès-de-Fenouillèdes 1972

Translated by Marie-Ange Chevrier
Dedicated to the memory of George Vayre
with thanks to his widow Denise and his family

Caudiès-de-Fenouillèdes

Chapter 16
MICHEL ROQUEBERT

Translated extracts from 'LES CATHARES ET LE GRAAL'

The God of Perceval is amazingly intimate. Familiar to man, His presence is constant, it is manifest at every turn of each adventure, by a voice, a sign, an image, a symbol, an allegory, it irrigates the entire world, creation and creatures, and gives meaning to the adventures. Nothing happens that could not be of God, not one event, the meaning of which is not in reference to it, be it as the realisation of His will or in opposition to it. Page after page God walks with those who seek Him, and they seek Him only because He is already there, present to all, but each wants to meet Him personally, through a concrete experience, a unique and implacable act of love.

God in Catharism is different. The unyielding opposition comes from the fact that He is fundamentally the God of the Gnostics, the very same ones whom as early as the 2nd century - therefore much earlier than the rise of Manichμism, which some would make the Cathars heir to - Irénée of Lyon condemns because: " . . . they turn away from He who He who ordered and created the Universe, as if they could find anything greater or higher than the God who created sky, earth and all who dwell therein!" For the Cathars, God is precisely this "greater or higher something."

It is necessary to find more solid ground and to ponder possible reciprocal influences between the Cathar religion and the discourse of the Grail. The tails of the Grail and Catharism certainly have in common that they offered to men, of the same epoch and same culture, a purifying process, an asceticism which in both cases could be taken as a path to initiation.

They were neither the first, nor the only ones to offer such a process of purification, but the parallels between the two approaches do deserve reflection, as well as the simultaneous nature of their emergence, even though the creation of Cathar doctrine largely predates the rising of Grail discourse and that they travelled together, so to speak, for only about forty years.

The two series of events - Romanesque development of Legend of the Grail and repression of Catharism - are exactly synchronous. However, he very essence of the Grail is that it was dreamed up, whereas the essence of Catharism is that it was lived.

THE DISCOURSE AND THE TEXT

It is beside the point, to list here all the pseudo-historic or literary theories that have, since the last century, presented very poetic parallels between Grail and Catharism, and which are apt to fire the imagination, but nonetheless, one can find no real justification, either in fact or in any written texts.

This is not to say that the study of the genesis and development this strange obsession (which at its most extreme identifies the treasure of the Grail and that of Montségur as one and the same, thus propelling thousands of tourists to look for traces of it in the ruins of the castle in the Ariège) is without interest, far from it. But this would be the work of the historian of literature, of myth or of the collective unconscious, rather than that of the factual historian. For the latter, the parallels present a fundamental problem. To consider that Perceval could be a figurative representation of Cathar religion; to believe the procession of the Grail could be a coded description of Cathar liturgy, on the pretext that it is not orthodox and does not correspond to any rituals of the Roman Catholic church; to imagine, more widely, that there could be found in the work of Chrétien de Troyes even as much as a shadow of the heretical message; all of this means totally ignoring the real conditions under which the work came into existence.

It has been abundantly demonstrated, that the Cathar heresy had certainly penetrated, in that same period, into Champagne and Flanders. But a region is not a milieu. The work of Chrétien was conceived, developed and written within a specific society, within the dominant aristocracy and intelligentsia, who were eminently orthodox. It can even be demonstrated that earlier, its patron, Marie de Champagne, to whom the work is dedicated, had made herself a name, in the chronicles, as an active persecutor of heretics.

FROM ADVENTURE TO QUEST

In 'The Booty of Annwfu', the thirtieth poem of the 'Book of Taliesin' (named after a Welsh bard of the 6th century), Arthur himself organises an expedition to take a mysterious far away city, where there is a cauldron of abundance, which never boils for the coward. The seeking of such talismans invariably requires a warlike venture of daring, endurance and heroism. We can observe in this, the fantasies of a precarious society, prey to permanent clan rivalries, and dreaming of a magical means to overcome hostility and survive. It is understandable that the rewriting of such themes, in the twelfth and thirteenth centuries, by Christian Occidental poets, for an audience of knights, eager for marvellous and heroic adventures, would have been undertaken for the purposes of spiritualism and sublimation. These talismans became mysterious objects, with Christian connotations, relics of Christ's Passion; the skills required to conquer them were not strictly warlike anymore, but had evolved into real virtues: faith, charity, purity. The longing for salvation replaced the appetite for power. The notion of eternal life replace that of earthly survival. Enemies were not seen anymore as neighbouring clans, but had become the emanations of evil, or even the Devil himself. In short, the conquering adventure had become an inner and spiritual one. In the final analysis, the first enemy one meets on the path is oneself and the adventure - which had now become the Quest - can only succeed through a total transcendence of the self by means of fasting and purification, at the end of which, ultimate revelations will come to pass: enlightenment to the mystical vision of the Grail.

Extracts from 'Les Cathares et le Graal' by Michel Roquebert
Published by Editions Privat, Toulouse, 1994
Translated by Marie-Ange Chevrier

The Theology of the Two Principles
Edited extract from 'LA RELIGION CATHARE'

Now the Cathars could not conceive of one Being having been able to create the incorruptible Kingdom, where there is no place for Evil, and the transient world, where evil abounds. This, then, presupposes two distinct and opposing creator-principles.

This fundamental belief of Catharism appeals for three types of argument:

i.   An argument of pure formal logic, taken from Aristotle: "The principles of the opposite are the opposite. Now Good and Evil are opposites. Therefore, they contain opposite principles." And to echo this argument, the Cathars quote St Matthew's Gospel: "Every corrupt tree bringeth forth evil fruit. A good tree cannot bring forth evil fruit, neither can a corrupt tree bring forth good fruit."

ii.   A scriptural argument, that is, taken from the Scriptures, here the third verse of the beginning of St John's Gospel: "Per ipsum omnia facta sunt, et sine ipso nihil factum est." The Catholics translate this as: "All things were made by Him and without Him was not one thing made." This pleonasm was challenged by the Cathars. They translate t as: "Without Him, Nothingness was made." Which is to say, obviously, the viable World. An interpretation that gives rise to much controversy in order to ascertain whether the Latin 'nihil', adverb of negation, could also be used as a noun. Not so, said the Catholics. Yes, said the Cathars, who found many an example in the New Testament. But they stumbled over one difficulty: John said that God created 'everything'; how can you have another creation that has been carried out without Him - even if it were that of 'nothingness'? The Cathar interpretation of this was that 'everything' does not always have the same meaning in the New Testament. When John says that God created 'everything', it had to be understood that as the invisibility and totality of the Good Creation (omnia invisibilia), but that there also is a visible totality (omnia visiblia) which God did not create. The proof is in the Scriptures: "All is vanity"; so it cannot refer to the same 'everything', because God could not have created a vain totality. Therefore there is an evil creation, which has its own principle.

iii.   An existential argument, that of the quasi-visceral refusal - over which no reasoned argument has any sway - to believe that an infinitely good God could have created conditions that allowed Evil to exist, in the form of matter and time, in other words, the World. For Catholics, God is all powerful and Evil could be a part of His secret design. The Cathars somehow invert the hierarchy of divine attributes. Of course God is Almighty, they say, but in 'good' alone, because His all powerfulness is limited by his infinite goodness. Since He is Love, He cannot be Evil, without contradicting or denying Himself.

It must be pre-supposed, then, in the theological argument of the Cathars, that there is a creator-principle of the World, where evil happens, which is separate from God. This principle is 'not-created' and is 'co-eternal' with the good God. But he is not a 'True God'. Of course, he is sometimes called the 'unknown God', but he could in no way be considered to be on the same level as the other. He is the Prince of the World, the Prince of Darkness, the Wicked Enemy. But he does not have Absolute existence, which belongs only to the True God. He is the negative, corrupt, destructive principle, never 'the Creator' in the real sense. And his own 'creations' must be understood as the permanent experiment of the destruction of the Good Creation. Confronted with the Spirit, he 'invents' Matter, in order to make the Spirit fall. Faced with Eternity, he 'invents' Time, so that everything becomes tainted throughout duration. In brief, his aim is that the Kingdom would be destroyed, be annihilated in the World. It is a purely 'reduced-to-nothingness' force, which is opposed to God, is somehow His reverse side, but not His equal, neither in value, nor in Being.

Thus, it was, the Cathars perceived the experiences of Evil and most especially its 'weightiness'.

Edited from 'LA RELIGION CATHARES' by Michel Roquebert
Editions Loubatieres, Toulouse, 1988; translation by Audrey Wagner

Chapter 17
YVES ROUQUETTE
Translated extract from 'CATHARES'

Are *you* a Cathar?

Joseph Delteil it was who first asked me the question nearly twenty years ago. I had just brought to him my translation into Occitan of his 'Jésus II'. He leant forward and, looking me straight in the eye, said: "Tell me, are *you* a Cathar?"

"No, I'm not."

"How can you say that? How can anyone not be a Cathar?"

Some years later, he returned to the charge. He sent us a copy of his 'Eloge de Clémence Isaure', and had written inside: "Yves, Marie, are you Cathars?" And still the answer was no.

I'm struck by how many people have that reaction. You tell them about the men and women who died in prison or at the stake for their faith in a God the father of good spirits, men and women who refused to see him as the creator of the world, of plants, animals and human beings. And your listeners only want to know, not only if there is a Cathar church now, some seven hundred years later, but also if you are a member. Again and again I have been asked the same question, after giving a talk, or by readers of mine, a question inspired, it seems, less by curiosity than by hope. I often used to dream of a Church of good spirits that had been revived and lived on, unobtrusively, or even in secret. To it would belong most of the writers whose books, poems, research or histories had revealed to me a special way of seeing God, fate and love. One would be René Nelli, because of his poems and his Journal spirituel d'un cathare d'aujourd'hui; another, of course, would be Déodat Roché; and Ferdnand Niel who thought Montségur was a solar temple; and Denis Saurat and his amazing poem Encaminament catar, 'Cathar Way':

> 'Ac digas pas; la jòia es amb nosaus',
> 'Say it not; joy is with us'

But there is no such Church. Déodat Roché was adamant; so was René Nelli, who became a friend. One evening a Réalmont, someone asked if there was a Cathar sect still active, and his answer was unambiguous:

"An active Cathar sect? The descendant of the Apostles by transmission of their authority and of divine influence? No. At least not to my knowledge."

There was, he said, a learned society, of which he was a member and which he and Déodat Roché had founded, but it was neither a church nor a sect. In the Société du Souvenir Cathare, later called Société des Etudes Cathares, the only members were searchers after historical truth, guardians of a memory, who had no intention of forming a Church.

I can vouch for the truth of that. Enthusiasts for mystery religions will have to face the facts. The men and women who earlier this century rescued Catharism from oblivion, and their successors, like Jean Duvernoy, Michel Roquebert and Anne Brenon, were not and are not the priests of a revived Cathar religion.

They were indeed scandalised by the drama of the Crusade, but dedicated themselves to research and publication only. They did not only throw light on what happened; we are indebted to them for what they have told us about the view of the world, God and salvation that made the Cathars first a special type of Christian, then 'heretics', and finally hunted animals and victims of persecution. As they worked on the texts they had rediscovered and analysed them in detail over time, they could obviously in most cases not remain unaltered in their ways of thinking, living or even creating. René Nelli's poems are, just as much as his essays, the proof that the philosophy and morality of the Good Men are still topical. But there are no perfecti or perfectµ today, carrying on from the twelfth, thirteenth and fourteenth centuries the 'Church of God'. That Church is dead and gone, and there is no sign that it will ever live again.

But, yes, I am a Cathar.

At least as much and as little as one can be in the 1990s; as much and as little as a man of meagre faith and slender hope can dare to claim, yes, I suppose I am a Cathar.

Did it take death to enlighten my darkened heart? Perhaps. Roché is dead; Nelli is dead; Jean Malrieu, another poet, and a communist, who found the understanding of fate on the road to Somplessac, is dead too. Of the three, it was René Nelli I was closest to, and I feel that death has hardly drawn us apart. It is thanks to him that today I believe and pray as a Cathar once did. I, a poor sinner, riddled with Roman Catholicism.

I believe in two principles. Or rather I believe, as we say in French, with a charcoal-burner's simple faith - for faith can only be dark, smoky, sooty - in a God of goodness who is all spirit and all love, and I refuse to trust in the other, who programmed, and still programs, the material universe in all its temporary splendour.

I pray to our father every day, hoping that He will be there at the end of my journey, waiting for me, and I thank Him for the mansions He has ready for us. Who is this Father? I am nor sure I know. I suppose He has the face you see on Russian icons of the Holy Face of Christ - the face of an unknowable God who cannot be seen by our eyes of flesh, our muscle-bound, moody minds: timeless, pure and simple love.

... ...

Of all the perfecti recorded in the inquisitor's registers, my favourite by far is William Belibaste. Probably because he was the last man to receive the consolamentum of ordination. His tragic death brought to an end more than two centuries of faith, of life in God, of hope.

Another reason is surely that he is more pitiful than exemplary, and yet in an ordinary and heroic way, the most imperfect of the known perfecti, the one whose earthly life gets through to the deepest, darkest, most loving side of me. No other among the dead has caused me to day-dream as long and as often as he has. It happens anywhere, anyhow, at any time - in the street, while friends are laughing, when sleep is slow to come.

None of it makes any sense, but I recognise myself in him.

Because he was born at Cubières, Belibaste came under the jurisdiction of the archbishop of Narbonne, to whom he was handed over and who ordered him to be executed in one of his possessions, the castle of Villerouge in the Pays de Termes.

Villerouge-Termenès is an attractive village in the plain, with many houses of russet stone and a castle that has been rebuilt a fair amount since those days, but it is still standing and looks the part. An engraved slab in the courtyard recalls the death of the last perfectus. That would have been enough: an inscription in angular letters and the same cross you find at Montségur and on Déodat Roché's grave.

But you could not expect the tourist trade to miss out on it. The vogue for Medieval pageants and mummery has not passed Villerouge by. The whole village has re-enacted Belibaste's burning at the stake for several years now, for he is their most famous son.

I have seen the olour photographs in the press. The Catholic warriors have tin helmets, painted wooden swords and drip-dry tunics. The Inquisitors have no difficulty disguising themselves as Dominicans, now that the monks have given up the cowl for three-piece suits. The horses are dressed up in the right sort of harness. The fellow playing Belibaste looks like one of Rodin's Burghers of Calais. They haul him to the stake, like Joan of Arc, light the fireworks and start the smoke machines. Then there is a Medieval banquet with wild boar and wenches, or perhaps just steak and chips and a bottle of Corbières.

There are people I trust, who say I am wrong to be so indignant. They say that within a few years Villerouge-Termenès has become one of the places where the martyrdom of the Cathars, and non-conformist Christians in general, is presented with seriousness and sincerity. They say that the pageant is nothing like the dreadful Medieval rubbish you find everywhere these days. I am glad to hear it. I shall go and see one day.

But when I first heard of it, I was so disgusted that I swore I would never set foot in Villerouge again. And then, every year, I found myself going back. Out of season, of course, but again and again.

Extract from 'Cathares' by Yves Rouquette
Loubatières, Tonlonse, 1992.
Translated by Roger Depledge

Villerouge-Termenès

PART FOUR: AFTER THE FIRE

Chapter 19
AFTER THE FIRE - INQUISITION!

The main purge of the Cathars, of the Perfecti, the believers and the supporters, took place between the start of the Albigensian Crusade in 1208 and the end of the siege of Montségur in 1244. During this period the cream of the Cathar church had been wiped out, with most of the church leaders and dedicated followers burned alive, often at mass public burnings.

Some mass burnings have been highlighted elsewhere in this book, Minerve, Lavaur and Montségur, being the most celebrated, the most fabled, but there were literally hundreds of others, with thousands of Cathars and Cathar supporters being burned at the stake. Fire seemed to symbolise the purge. A clean, efficient and portentous means of execution. For the Catholic church, these burnings were a visible symbol of the churches authority and power, at the same time, reminding the any reluctant or reticent Catholics present of the hell-fire awaiting them should they stray from the safety of the church, and associating those burned with the Devil himself.

It is hard for us to imagine it now, being burned alive. The sounds - sizzling as the liquid parts of the body boil, popping of the blistered flesh, the roar of the flames. The smell of burning wood, of cooking flesh. The horrific sight as the body is stripped of its skin, its fatty tissue, its exposed organs and as the searing flames rap around the white skeletal bones. Think of that, on a mass scale, regularly carried out. Think of that and think that, despite the dangers of such consequences, people still retained their Cathar faith.

Although the major purge took place within the 1208 to 1244 period, the earliest recorded burnings of `Cathars` are at Orléans and Toulouse, as early as 1002. Such executions became more common after the Cathar church had decided to `come out`, with the Cathar Council of St Félix-de-Caraman in 1167. And the persecution of Cathar sympathisers was to carry on until well into the fourteenth century.

If the first part of this three hundred year persecution was dominated by the burning pyres, the second part was dominated by a new, even more sinister institution, the Inquisition.

The Inquisition, as it established itself in this region, was seventy-five years of interrogations, trials and sentences. There were relatively few burnings, as compared to the fires lit by Simon de Montfort, in the single year of 1210. But there were many imprisonments, tortures, confiscations, and people sent into exile. Above all, there was profound disturbance in the ranks of believers, consumed by fear and denouncement. Yet faith remained pure and ardent. It would be a mistake to suppose that Catharism, as it was being finally eliminated, was contaminated and decadent. However, the circle of Bons-Hommes and Bonnes-Dames was gradually and inexorably being narrowed.

It fell to the comparatively newly established orders of Dominicans and Franciscans to undertake the process of the Inquisition. The irony of this is that the founders of these orders, St Dominic and St Francis, had both admired certain aspects of the Cathar religion, particularly the giving up of worldly possessions in order to dedicate oneself fully to the works of God. Both had enjoyed the theological debates with the Cathar ministers and respected the sincerity of their belief, if not its principles. Now, as the agents of the Inquisition, Dominican and the Franciscan monks were required to persuade neighbour to betray neighbour, to use fear to acquire confession, and to condemn often innocent people to mental and physical torture, often to the death.

The monks devoutly believed that they were involved in the Inquisition in order to save souls from damnation. In all sincerity they used the strength of their own faith to push themselves in carrying out the inquisitorial processes with rigorous conviction, often imposing intolerable pressure on those unfortunates who came before them. But it was their mission to root out 'heresy', wherever it might be hiding, to cleanse the region of faltering or misguided belief, to bring people back to the fold. In this processes the end justified the means - any means!

Historians have pounced on the Inquisition with researchers' glee. For the one thing the Inquisition did do was to keep records. One of the principal sources of information about the Cathars has been the registers of the Inquisition. In other words, much, if not most, of our evidence about the doctrine and the religious system of the Cathars is based on information derived from the Catholic church, which had exterminated Catharism as a dangerous rival. There is no doubt that the impartiality of such sources must be suspect, since those collecting the information had acted as judge, jury and executioner in the process of investigation.

It is also important to bear in mind that the material gathered by the Inquisition and contained in its registers is of a comparatively late date. Such material represents Catharism when it was much weakened by almost two centuries of savage persecution and when it was undergoing a process of corruption and denigration almost inseparable from persecution. The most prominent ministers of the Cathar church had already perished during the years of crusade, and the interrogations which have come down to us are primarily those from people 'suspected' of Cathar 'heresy', of mere 'possible credents'. These were mostly peasant people, ignorant of the theological arguments, easily falling into the traps that were being laid for them in the questioning, holding many half-understood views, were confused and inconsistent under skilled cross-examination, and they were scared. On their testimony could depend their own fate, as well as that of family, relatives and friends. As Bernard Delicios, the prominent Franciscan critic of the Inquisition, said:

"The Apostles Peter and Paul, if brought before the Inquisition, would scarcely be able to justify themselves. It is no longer a matter of justice, when interrogation has become the subtle art of setting traps, into which guilty and innocent stumble, alike."

The reason historians have been so enthusiastic about the records of the Inquisition, is that there were so many of them. The Inquisition records in the in the libraries of Toulouse and Carcassonne show that a complete inventory was made, even in the most remote and tiniest of hamlets, of beliefs, doctrines, organisation, and activity of the Cathars over the preceding half century. One inquisitor alone examined no fewer than 5638 sworn witnesses. That much of the information, gathered on such a vast scale, made in different times and places, substantially concurs, has been taken by some historians to mean that reasonable reconstructions can be based on these records. After all, the main aim of the enquiry was to obtain information, and neither the inquisitors nor the Catholic church had any interest in obtaining false answers, nor with charging 'heretics' with beliefs they did not hold.

Even if we admit that the inquisitors, and the Catholic historians, were fair, balanced and scientific in their handling of these records, the dogmatic doctrinal convictions of the questioners and the fear and insecurities of the witnesses must cast a shadow of doubt over any such material. We should review it with caution. Moreover, it must never be forgotten that this emphasis of doctrinal difference only arises because the Catholic church triumphed. Prominent theologians in the Catholic church admitted that the morals and conduct of the Cathar Perfecti were exemplary. Therefore, they could not be attacked on these grounds. Instead, the attack was mounted on doctrinal extravagances. But the whole point of Catharism was in their conception that Christianity is a life lived, not a doctrine believed in - *"Do as I do, not as I say."* For them, the life of Jesus was a model that the good Christian should aspire to, not a cosmic mystery to be blindly accepted on trust.

Even after the horrors of the Crusade, and the severity of the persecutions, Catharism still showed signs of life. Instead of being openly practised in the traditional form, at Cathar 'houses', it was forced underground and was conducted in a clandestine way. The Perfecti no longer wore beards, or dressed in the dark habits, but they carried their New Testament and Cathar texts in a pouch, strapped around the chest, and hidden under normal clothing. Cathar leaders and followers spread out into the mountainous countryside, into the

Fenouillèdes, into the Corbiéres, into higher and far flung reaches of the Pyrénées. It was into these mountain communities that the Catholic Inquisition largely concentrated its efforts.

One of the most extensive recordings of an inquisitional court was that carried out by Jacques Fournier, Bishop of Pamiers and later to become Pope Benedict XII, in which people of small villages in the Ariège district, primarily from Montaillou, were examined. The text of this has been published in its entirety by Jean Duvernoy as 'Le Registre d'Inquisition de Jacques Fournier, evéque de Pamiers (1318-1325), but a more popular résumé of the findings of Fournier's court was published by Emmanuel Le Roy Ladurie in 1978, under the title Montaillou: village occitan de 1294 - 1324. This gives an extraordinary detailed and vivid picture of the everyday life of the people in this small Medieval village. Fournier and his team of inquisitors were determined to flush out the last pockets of Cathar resistance, in places like Montaillou. By means of a detailed enquiry of individuals, they were either able to bring people back into the Catholic fold or to condemn them as 'heretics'. Some of these were burned at the stake, many were sentenced to imprisonment, even more were condemned to wear the yellow cross. Just as Medieval Jews were compelled to wear a yellow star (and what contemporary resonances does that make?), so condemned 'heretics' were compelled to wear on their backs large crosses made from material sown to their outer garments.

Jacques Fournier was recognised as obsessional and fanatical in his pursuit of all kinds of 'suspects'. When he became Bishop of Pamiers, in 1317, he took advantage of a dictum of the Council of Vienna, which stipulated that the powers of the local Bishop were to be used in support of the Dominican officials in charge of the Inquisition in their region. So in the following year, Fournier set up his own Office of the Inquisition in Pamiers. As an inquisitor, he regarded himself as immune both to supplication and to bribe, as skilful at 'worming out the truth, in order to bring the lambs forth', and that he had the ability to tell, after a few minutes, a 'heretic' from a 'proper' Catholic. He was 'the very Devil of an Inquisitor', to those that he accused.

He succeeded, largely, through the diabolical and tenacious skill of his interrogations, only rarely having to resort to torture. He was fanatical about detail and was present, in person, at almost every sitting of his court, wanting to direct everything himself, refusing to delegate responsibility to subordinates, scribes and notaries.

Fournier's court met at Pamiers and worked for 370 days, carrying out some 578 interrogations. They dealt with ninety-eight cases of 'suspected heresy' involving in total some 114 people, of which around thirty came from the village of Montaillou, others from surrounding districts. From the extensive records of these court proceedings investigating the people of Montaillou, the most striking feature is the simple nature of the village life that these people led, ordinary in the extreme. In their beliefs, almost all the people of the village, including the local priest, had been influenced, to some extent or other, by the Bons-Hommes and Bonnes-Dames, who had been in their midst, lived and worked amongst them.

The shepherds of Montaillou had become fond of discussing theology, even though some of the Cathar sympathisers were a little uncertain on several points of doctrine. The frontiers between the believers in Catharism and believers in orthodox Catholic faith was vague, and easily crossed in both directions, by the same people. Much depended on the natural changing networks of friendly or working relationships between individuals. For example, from the record of the interrogation of Pierre Maury, a shepherd:

"I want to use what I earn from my work to do good on both sides. Because I really do not know which of the two beliefs is more valid. Although, in fact, I rather support the faith of the heretics. But that is simply because my communications and relations with the heretics are greater than with the others."

We learn intimate details of the villagers lives, like the unfortunate Béatrice, widowed from a series of marriages, many of them loveless and unsatisfactory, raped by the brother of the local priest, and eventually falling in love with the priest, Pierre Clergue, and being publicly kept by him. She was condemned to wear the double yellow cross.

The accused usually spoke in Occitan, or in a few cases in Gascon. The scribes translated the words into Latin, for the records, as the notes were being taken, a sort of 'simultaneous translation'. A spoken translation back into the 'vulgar tongue' was made, when reading back to the accused, so they could make any additions or alterations they felt necessary.

All the evidence of Fournier's register suggests that in Montaillou, those who believed in the myth and ritual of Catharism experienced it as an extreme and heroic variant of Christianity, not as a non-Christian religion. The Cathar believers were convinced in their heart of hearts that they were Christians, which in fact they were. Jacques Fournier's Inquisition Register is a factual history of ordinary people. It is Pierre Maury and his flock of sheep, it is the story of Pierre and Béatrice, as lovers, it is an everyday story of countryfolk, going about their daily business and trying, at the edges of it, to make sense of being in this world.

For this latter sin, some were imprisoned, for varying degrees of strictness, some were sent on pilgrimages and had their goods confiscated, some were compelled to wear the yellow cross in all public situations.

Five were burned at the stake.

It was in the land of Aude that the final scene of the Cathar tragedy was enacted. As Yves Rouquette recounted earlier, the last Cathar Perfectus was a man called Guillaume Bélibaste. Born in the village of Cubières sur Cinoble, Bélibaste was not a particularly 'good' Perfectus, and he knew it. He was something of a simple, old bluffer, who had started as a nomad shepherd and was ordained without a vocation, having once killed a man in a bar-room brawl.

He was ostensibly the last Cathar to receive the Consolamentum, and consequently had the power to transmit it. There was a fierce determination on the part of the Inquisition to get hold of old Bélibaste, for his death would break the 'Apostolic chain' and for lack of sacraments, there would never more be any Parfaits or Parfaites.

The officers of the Inquisition deployed a wealth of unsavoury tricks, until one of their spies finally revealed the whereabouts of Bélibaste, forcing him out of hiding. As a subject of the archbishop of Narbonne, he was burnt to death in the autumn of 1321, on the archbishop's own estate at Viellerouge, not far from the château of Termes.

... .

So, was the death of Bélibaste the end of Catharism?

As Yves Rouquette has pointed out, people like René Nelli, Déodat Roché, and dedicated Occitanian poets, revived the interest in Catharism in the 1930s. Yves Rouquette has continued this excellent work. And Jean Duvernoy has delved deep into the records of the Inquisition to try to find out what made the followers of Catharism still so doggedly to their beliefs, despite the horrors heaped upon them. A later grouping of seekers after the truth about the Good People helped establish the Centre for the Study of Catharism, aptly named the René Nelli Centre, for many years based at the Château at Villegly, but now moved to Carcassonne. Anne Brenon, Nicolas Gouzy, Michel Roquebert, Jean-Louis Gasc, whose excellent photographs capture the very spirit of Catharism.

Outside of France, Arthur Guirdham, a distinguished psychiatrist, became involved in regression to former lives, after discovering that he may, himself, have been a Cathar in a previous existence. He now claims to have made contact with a wide range of people, all of whom remember intimate details of their life during the Albigensian Crusdae and Inquisition.

Baigent, Leigh and Lincoln launched all manner of seekers off to southern France, when they published details of Holy bloodlines and possible treasure. Many people in the Languedoc region regard this as a mixed blessing, but their best-selling book has no doubt helped to engaged the interest of many, many people in the Cathars and related matters. Henry Lincoln is now heavily engaged in research to find out why the area around Rennes-le-Château and

Rennes-le-Bains might have been the site of a huge temple in times prehistory.

Michael Bradley has documented a trail of the Cathars into Novia Scotia and Newfoundland and Ken Campbell, a regular visitor to those shores, has recently made contact with the family Le Blanc, who are probably direct descendents of Cathars, with a strong interest in retaining Catharist principles.

Whilst I was typing one draft of this book, the Prince of Wales, our much troubled, possible future monarch, was being interviewed on the radio. He said:

"Religion means 'to bind'......resolving the inner conflict between the light and the dark."

Gives you food for thought, doesn't it?

The Cathedral at Albi - this is the sort of church you build when you want to show that you have won!

Chapter 20
DOES CATHARISM DISSOLVE IN PRINTING INK?

Nicolas Gouzy, Director of the Centre Etudes Cathares, introduces a selected bibliography.

Under this provocative title I propose to invite you on a rapid, but nonetheless earnest tour of what visitors to our region can expect to find in the way of information on the subject. What is there on the market to guide an honest approach to Catharism and its context?

In assembling this short bibliography, I have used the facilities provided by the library of the Centre Etudes Cathares, my personal experience as a researcher and a few afternoons in the most popular tourist bookshops in the area. I have also drawn upon inquiries carried out by the main libraries of the South of France and have trusted to my own understanding of the motivations of people visiting our part of the country, who are bound to take an interest in the Cathars, to some extent or other.

Aué, Michèle; Cathar Country (MSM, Vic-en-Bigorre, 1992)

Aubarbier, Jean-Luc; Wonderful Cathar Country (Editions Ouest-France, Rennes, 1194)

Baigent, Michael, Leigh, Richard & Lincoln, Henry; The Holy Blood and the Holy Grail (Cape, London, 1982; Corgi, Ealing, 1991)

Borst, Arno; Die Katharer (Schriften der Monumenta Germani`historica, Stuttgart, 1953)

Brenon, Anne; La Vrai Visage du Catharisme (Loubatières, Toulouse, 1991)

Brenon, Anne; Les Femmes Cathares (Perrin, Paris, 1994)

Duvernoy, Jean;. Le Catharisme: la Religion des Cathares (Privat, Toulouse, 1976) 2 vols.

Duvernoy, Jean, ed. Registres d'inquisition de Jacques Fournier; annotated translation into French of the Inquisition records from Pamiers, 1318-1325 (Mouton, Paris, 1978) 3 vols

Gougaud, Henri; Bélibaste - a novel based on the last Cathar Perfecti (Editions du Seuil, Paris, 1982)

Hamilton, Bernard; The Albigensian Crusade (Historical Assoc., London, 1974)

Ladurie, Emmanuel Le Roy; Montaillou: village Occitan, 1294-1324 (Gallimard, Paris, 1975; Penguin, London, 1978)

Martin-Chabot, Eugène, trans.,ed.; La Chanson de la Croisade Albigeois, translation from the 13th century account in the original Occitan, one of the few remaining contemporary records (Belles Lettres, Paris 1976) 3 vols

Neil, Fernand; Les Cathares de Montségur (Paris, 1978)

Nelli, René; La Vie Quotidenne des Cathares du Languedoc au XIIIᵉ siècle (Paris, 1969)

Nelli, René; Ecritures Cathares: textes prèCathares et Cathares (Paris, 1968)

Oblensky, D.; The Bogomils: a study of Balkan neo-Manichæism (Twickenham, 1972)

Oldenburg, Zoe; Massacre at Montségur: a history of the Albigensian Crusade (New York,1961)

Peyrat, Nicholas, Histoire des Albigeois (Paris, 1870-2) 3 vols.

Roché, Déodat, Le Catharisme (Toulouse, 1947)

Roquebert, Michel; L'Epopee Cathares (Privat, Toulouse, 1971-1994) 5 vols.

Roquebert, Michel, Le Cathare et le Graal (Privat, Toulouse, 1994)

Roquebert, Michel & Bibollet, Catherine; Light and Shade in the Country of the Cathars (Privat, Toulouse, 1992)

Rouquette, Yves; Cathars. (Loubatières, Toulouse, English edition, 1992)

Runciman, Sir Stephen; The Medieval Manichee: a study of Christian dualist heresy (Cambridge, 1947)

Sumption, Jonathan; The Albigensian Crusade (Faber, London, 1978)

Thouzellier, C.; Rituel Cathare: texte critique, traduction et notes (Paris, 1977)

Wakefield, Walter; Heresy, Crusade and Inquisition in Southern France, 1100-1250 (New York,1974)

Wakefield, Walter & Evans, Austin; Heresies of the Middle Ages (New York, 1991)

Editions Loubatières have a series of booklets in a range of languages covering subjects related to Cathars and Catharism, the following are particularly recommended:

Cathar Castles by Georges Serrus & Michel Roquebert

Cathar Religion by Michel Roquebert

Montségur by Georges Serrus

Occitanie, notre terre by Yves Rouquette

Minerve, Cite Cathare by Philip Assié

Les Cathares: Chronologie de 1022-1321; a comprehensive pack of maps and detailed information covering the major incidents in the Albigensian Crusade and other relevant material, the intricate details of provinces, monarchies, political situation, etc. (Griffe, Cagnes, 1991)

Heresis - Revue d'Heresiologie Medieval, textes, recherche; review of contemporary research, published regularly by Centre Etude Cathares, Carcassonne.

Cahiers d'Etude Cathares; published from Arques since 1949, quarterly.

Cahiers de Fanjeaux; published from Toulouse since 1966, quarterly.

Additional Related Reading Material

In addition to Nicolas Gouzy's excellent selection above, I would also recommend the following books to follow up related matters covered in this book:

Armstrong, Karen; Holy War, the Crusades and their impact on today's world (Channel 4 Books, London, 1988)

Bradley, Michael; Holy Grail Across the Atlantic (Hounslow, Ontario, Canada, 1988)

Campbell, Ken; The Trilogy - Furtive Nudist, Pigspurt, Jamais Vu (Methuen, London, 1992-5)

Frayling, Christopher; Strange Landscape, a journey through the Middle Ages (BBC, London, 1995)

Guirdham, Arthur; Cathars and Reincarnation (Spearman, Suffolk, 1970)

Guirdham, Arthur; The Great Heresy (Spearman, Suffolk, 1977; Daniel, Essex, 1993)

Riley-Smith, Jonathan; The Atlas of the Crusades (Times Books, London, 1991)

Ricciotti, Giuseppe; The Age of Martyrs - Christianity from Diocletian to Constantine (Barnes & Noble, New York, 1992

Roszak, Theodore; Flicker - the book that started it all, for me! (Bantam, London, 1992)

.....and no, Nicolas, printing ink does not dissolve Catharism, printing ink is very much helping to keep it alive!